What a lovely article about you and Marcy in Maui together! On the one hand, we mothers are grateful that we have beautiful memories of our child, but, on the other hand, we wish they were simply beautiful memories and not attached to the present absence of our beloved child. We go on; we thank God that we are still sane, and we are grateful for the daily courage to help the grieving world. Take good care of your heart, Sandy. You have work to do!

Mary Jane Hurley Brant, psychotherapist, grief specialist,
Bereaved parent and author of When Every Day Matters: A
Mother's Memoir on Love, Loss and Life

My 4-year-old son drowned while visiting at his father's house January 2009. Nothing could prepare me for the devastation, confusion, sorrow and pain that I feel. Your writings, although they make me cry, give me direction, hope and compassion. I don't feel so alone when reading them. Love and blessings from South Africa.

Alison Starbuck, bereaved mother

I attended The Compassionate Friends National Conference in 2007 and heard Sandy's workshop on Coping Strategies for surviving parents of only children. The workshop gave us encouragement and inspiration as we continue our difficult journey.

Neil Brenckman, bereaved father

I applaud you for your article on saying inappropriate things to bereaved parents. I'm so grateful for your articles. Just the other day I was told I need to "get over it," that life is passing me by. It left me with not wanting to let anyone know that I'm still grieving…I wrote a poem that reflects how angry I became because of those three words

Deborah Ann Tornillo, author of 36 Days Apart

Our only son passed away at age 21 in Sept. 2002. So much of what you have written truly hits home for me and, I know, for other parents who have experienced the death of a child. I had to write to thank you for your writings.

Carol Fox (1

What beautiful work you are doing with your articles to continue the memory of Marcy, as well as helping so many others with their grief. Although I never met Marcy, I remember her through you and was grateful I got to watch the video of her. I can see how she continues to touch others; her love and laughter still fill the hearts of those who remember her so lovingly. In gratitude and love for knowing you, and knowing Marcy. I feel blessed, honored and grateful.

Rev. Malika Lynn Pohjola

I lost my 15-year-old daughter December 2007 from a nine-month battle with cancer. I, like you, have pictures in each room of her, and as you, a box of special things in my closet I love to go through. I want to thank you for your writings. I also read your book *I Have No Intention of Saying Good-bye.*

Stephanie Jayebert, bereaved mother

Although I have not had a child die, I believe it is important to know what to say and how to help any friends who are going through the grief process. This book with so many coping techniques and strategies will help me do that. Thanks, Sandy.

Kate Simon

What you wrote: "Life goes on and others forget and move on. Not so for bereaved mothers." It is so true, so true…

Louise Lagerman, bereaved mother

My wife and I are dealing with the aftermath of our much beloved older son's death. During our last couples' therapy session, the 90% divorce rate was given as a fact… I found your article (on low divorce rates) really helpful. Thanks.

Carlos Luch, bereaved father

Creating a New Normal...After the Death of a Child

Sandy Fox

iUniverse, Inc.
New York   Bloomington

Creating a New Normal...After the Death of a Child

iUniverse books may be ordered through booksellers or by contacting:

iUniverse
1663 Liberty Drive
Bloomington, IN 47403
www.iuniverse.com
1-800-Authors (1-800-288-4677)

Because of the dynamic nature of the Internet, any Web addresses or links contained in this book may have changed since publication and may no longer be valid. The views expressed in this work are solely those of the author and do not necessarily reflect the views of the publisher, and the publisher hereby disclaims any responsibility for them.

ISBN: 978-1-4502-3094-0 (sc)
ISBN: 978-1-4502-3095-7 (ebook)

Printed in the United States of America

iUniverse rev. date: 6/4/2010

Other Published Books by Sandy Fox

*A Complete History of the Glendale Union
High School District*, 1978

I Have No Intention of Saying Good-bye, 2001

You Are in Every Sunrise

My child
You are gone from me physically
But I see your face.
You are in every sunrise
In every new bloom
In every new season.
I can hear your voice
I can hear your laughter
I remember it all so well.
It warms my heart
To think of you always
With wonderful memories.
My journey has been long and uncharted
I am amazed at where I am in this journey…
A new life, a new joy, a new love
But what I wouldn't give to have you back with me.
I know in my heart that can never be.
But it doesn't stop me
From wishing…
You are not forgotten
You will never be forgotten
I will see to it.
I will build memorials
So that others will learn and understand
Who you are, what you became
Through nurtured loved for so many years.
Our lives are shaped
As much by those who leave us
As they are by those who stay.
Your spirit is all around me
I can feel you
I can sense you
Stay with me always
Help me to put back
The pieces of the puzzle.

Mom

Contents

Acknowledgments

To all the bereaved parents I have spoken to and become friendly with in the years since Marcy died…I am forever grateful for your help. Your thoughts and ways of coping, your willingness to share your stories, and your hopes and dreams for the future for my first bereavement book *I Have No Intention of Saying Good-bye* and now for this new book *Creating A New Normal…After the Death of a Child* were of great help in these writings.

A special appreciation goes to the parents I interviewed for the 10 inspirational stories in this book and to the professional writers and bereavement specialists named, along with their works, within this book.

Lastly, a special thanks to my wonderful husband, Lawrence, who offered and did one of the final proofs of the book before printing.

And when we have remembered everything,
We grow afraid of what we may forget.
A face? A voice? A smile? A birthday? An anniversary?
No need to fear forgetting, because the heart remembers always.

Sascha Wagner

Dedication

For my beloved daughter, Marcy, and all the children who died too soon. You will not be forgotten.

Introduction

As I go through my never-ending grief journey, I have learned so much that I want to share with other bereaved parents in hopes that they, too, will benefit.

Our lives have changed so much since our child died. We are no longer the person we were before. We have new priorities and values, new goals and particularly, new friends. What was once important to us may no longer have any meaning. Now I brake to look at a beautiful sunset. I value people more than things. Moments are important. What we wished for our child's future is no longer important; he/she is gone. What we do now with *our* lives is what is important. We will have to rewrite our address books. Friends may not be able to deal with us; they will say we've changed. They are right; we have. How can we *not* change when we lose a child? We are overwhelmed with our unspeakable loss, angry, bewildered and frustrated. Our life has been turned upside down, and it's like having to start over again. All of these thoughts and others enter our minds and the solutions are not apparent at all.

When I picked up a piece of the shattered headlight from the car that my daughter died in many years ago, I thought, "This resembles my life now, smashed into a hundred pieces." What could I do to survive the present and regain goals for my future? In time, we all must answer those questions for ourselves and with the help of others.

From speaking at national bereavement conferences and various other organizations to writing my heart out in books on surviving grief, columns and articles for bereavement foundations and magazines, I have tried to get my message to others. That message is "You will find that the life you once knew with your child is over and you have to create a new normal for yourself in order to put back the pieces and start living again." Hence, the title of this new book: *Creating a New Normal...After the Death of a Child.*

How do you go about doing this? That is what this book is about: many coping and informational strategies in short article form that I have written. Parts of these articles have appeared on my personal blog, www.survivinggrief.blogspot.com, but most of the articles are new or expanded with additional information from myself and named professionals in the field. Along with the articles are inspirational personal stories from bereaved parents as well as some poetry, book recommendations, grief quotes, resources and comments from parents living through this nightmare. Everyone has different views as to how to go about doing this.

Don't think for one minute you will not have setbacks, not cry, not have to reach out to other, and not struggle for answers, because you will. We are all seeking and struggling to build a future for ourselves. This book gives many ideas and suggestions, but they are, by far, not the only ones. I encourage you to find other ideas in your quest to reach out and grow. I, too, will always be thirsty for knowledge and invite you to share your findings with me.

This book is written in short article form, so that each one can be read individually or a few at a time. You can come back to them or continue on to others as you wish. If you find some concepts overlapping, it is because it is relevant to that article. I also use many examples from my daughter's life to add to the relevancy of these articles, as well as give you some personal thoughts on daughter Marcy and myself in a separate section.

When you are done, I hope you will take the advice given in these written words, if you believe it will be of help to you. May you also be able to see the light at the end of the tunnel by creating your own new normal.

Sandy Fox
sfoxaz@hotmail.com
www.sandyfoxauthor.com

Part 1
General Coping Strategies
for the Bereaved

Within this section are 33 articles for those who are looking for useful techniques to help them cope with the death of a child. Whether you have lost one or more children or are seeking information to help a friend or relative, this section has an array of articles to help you. They deal with topics such as the stages of grief, teaching others about our grief, making a marriage work, how time plays a role in the grief process, inappropriate responses to bereaved parents, signs we get from our children and many more topics. You can learn many lessons by reading these articles. Use them to your advantage.

It is one of the most beautiful compensations of life that no man can sincerely try to help another without helping himself.

-Ralph Waldo Emerson

1.   Stages of Grief

In the first few years of our grief journey, we experience so many different emotions, all of which are normal and not "weird" as some people may say to us.

There are five phases of grief (some experts use different names for each phase, but in the end they are all the same). As I write about each, I will tell you how I personally fit into each one. Keep in mind that leaving one phase and moving on to another does not mean we will not return to that phase or overlap between phases. Going back and forth is normal. We will be able to deal with it all eventually, but don't expect too much of yourself at first and don't expect to move on too quickly. Your grief journey could take anywhere from one to five years or even longer. It all depends on how we handle each phase, each benchmark. Each phase offers an opportunity for growth. Facing this process takes courage and a willingness to want to get better.

STAGES OF GRIEF
- **Shock**
- **Awareness of loss**
- **Conservation/Withdrawal**
- **Healing**
- **Renewal**

The first phase is **SHOCK**. We can't believe this has happened. Children don't die before their parents. How the death occurred and whether it was a sudden death or anticipated death can determine how we first react. Screaming, shouting, feeling confused, being forgetful or so numb we can't function at all are some of the reactions.

My daughter's death was a sudden death, a car accident. I received a call at 11:30 p.m. and told. I couldn't believe what I was hearing. My daughter and her husband Simon were in a new car that was hit broadside. Marcy died instantly. (Simon, who was driving, survived but not before 20 life-threatening operations over a 13 year period.) No, this could not happen to my beautiful, intelligent daughter who was so enthusiastic about life. I remember being numb at first. I just wanted information, to know how it had happened, when and where, and then the thought came that perhaps this was just a cruel joke, so a call went out to the morgue. Yes, she was there, I heard someone say. Then the screams came. Everything became a blur, and I desperately wanted to make some sense out of what happened but could not. We never expect our children to die. We are so attached to them that part of us dies too. We also feel in some way we have failed and not protected them. At some point when the shock wears off, we begin to feel the intensity of our grief and move into the second phase.

In the second phase, **AWARENESS OF LOSS**, we experience intense emotions. We may feel like we are having a heart attack or trouble breathing deeply. Other signs of this phase include a sense of guilt that we did something to cause the death, frustration at not being able to save our child, and anger toward the person who was responsible.

I felt mostly anger. Police officers assumed an impaired male driver killed my child; empty beer cans littered the van. My anger began to build as the days and months wore on, and I kept saying to myself, "What a waste of a beautiful life!" I wanted the driver caught and punished. Eyewitnesses had police experts do a drawing of the man, but he was never found, causing the anger to last longer than I anticipated. Then another thought came—did I really want to go through a trial, have to sit there, have to look at a person who took my daughter's life. Just maybe, I was better off this way. It certainly helped ease the nightmares. Those thoughts are what pushed me through this phase.

Additional characteristics of this phase one might encounter include prolonged stress and physical anxiety like your heart beating very fast when thinking about the situation; oversensitivity at what people may say, do and not do; and a sense of security severely uprooted through stress which makes us feel vulnerable. Our bodies become exhausted and we begin to move into the next phase.

The third phase, **CONSERVATION/WITHDRAWAL,** can include fatigue, despair, a weakened immune system and hibernation. Many parents don't realize they are not getting enough rest and sleep. We may withdraw from friends and want to be alone with their thoughts. By this phase, we are exhausted with all that has happened and are in a time of dark despair because physical and emotional defenses are seriously diminished. We may find ourselves getting physically ill with the flu because our immune system is in a weakened state. Our body has used up all of our physical and emotional energy. We need to take care of ourselves and begin our grief work to get over the hump of this phase. Decide who we are now and what we are going to do with the rest of our lives.

Although I was lethargic and did not care about much of anything after my daughter died, I did not get physically ill. My blood sugar and blood pressure were up, but after visiting the doctor, he understood the cause, forced me to watch what I ate and encouraged me to exercise. I found exercising to be of great value to me. It relieved a lot of tension that had built up, and I truly believe exercise helped keep me well. After a while, I began to get back into a pattern of living a different kind of life without my daughter.

In the fourth phase, **HEALING**, we begin to take control of our life. We realize our old life is over forever and we must begin to find a new path, in essence form a new identity. We will lose some friends who can't deal with our loss but, in the process, find new ones who have experienced the loss of a child and want to share their thoughts and feelings with us. We may find a grief group in the area to join or grief recovery books to read.

I read everything I could get my hands on. That is not to say that I liked or agreed with everything I read, but different thoughts from others who were bereaved helped me to sort out my own feelings. I did not attend support group meetings. Although I did not mind telling my story, at the time I was not interested in hearing everyone else's problems at these meetings. I had enough of my own. Healing comes slowly; sometimes we don't realize it is happening. We may discover an interest in something new, we may feel more energetic, we may have to restructure the person we were before this happened to us. When we finally let go, our identity shifts, and we will be able to see our new life for what it is.

The last phase is **RENEWAL**. Those who have lost a child have to learn to live without them. It can take a very long time to get to the other side. Turning to the future, we realize we are not the same person we were before our child died. We have new priorities, new goals and a new compassion to share with others.

Learning to laugh again and not feel guilty for feeling good was to me a great gift that I hope to continue to share with others. This phase of renewal provides the opportunity to develop new self-awareness as well as emotional independence.

Take charge of your life. What I did was to become very involved with helping others who are grieving, by speaking to groups and letting them know they are not alone and that they will find their way eventually. I fulfilled an inner need that I had, and it gave me satisfaction to know I could be of help to others. In turn, helping others has been a catharsis for me. In helping others, we, indeed, help ourselves to find joy once again.

There is no way to predict how long our recovery will take. We have to learn much along the way before we can move through the process. We have to believe better times will come. I can personally tell you that they did for me, as I am sure they will for you.

2. Teaching Others About Our Grief and How They Can Help

We cannot expect others to understand how we feel after the death of a child, especially if they have never gone through it. Sometimes we get angry at how friends or relatives react and respond to us. They don't know what to say or how to say it and often they say it wrong, not meaning to be cruel, but not knowing any better.

We have a choice. We can be bitter and resentful to others, or we can help them understand us to be part of our grief journey. What follows are statements from those on their grief journey and how friends and relatives can respond to us. By sharing these thoughts with those close to you, a new level of understanding between everyone can help you down that long difficult road to recovery.

- **BE THERE FOR ME**. If you are my friend, reach out, talk to me, hold my hand and hug me. Know that even though we may say we are all right, we will never be all right again. Have that shoulder ready for me to cry on. At any moment, I can lose control of my emotions for any reason: a song on the radio, a birthday I can no longer share or a special holiday. Being silent with each other is okay. Saying, "I'm sorry" is simple, but says more than anything else can at a time like this.

- **WE ARE DIFFERENT**. Understand that what has happened will change us forever and if you are my friend, you will accept me for what I have become, for who I am now, a person with different goals and different priorities. What was once important to me may no longer have any meaning.

- **BE A GOOD LISTENER.** We want above all else to talk about our children. To us, they will always be alive in our hearts, and we don't want others to forget them either. Don't be afraid to mention their names in our conversations. They were real people at one time, even though they are no longer with us. They had hopes and dreams we would still like to share with others. Please don't pretend they never existed. Encourage me to talk about my child and truly hear what I have to say. You may also learn something you never knew that could be of help in how you react to me.

- **NO ONE ELSE KNOWS HOW I FEEL.** We all grieve differently, even husbands and wives. Please don't tell me you know how I feel. You don't. Rather than asking me, "How are you feeling?" ask me "What are you feeling?" I can probably give you a more honest answer.

- **I MAY GRIEVE FOR A VERY LONG TIME.** There is no set time limit to my grief. It may take me two years; it may take me five years. I have to do what is comfortable for me. Be patient. I will do the best I can in whatever amount of time it takes.

- **KEEP IN TOUCH.** Call me occasionally. I promise to do the same. Invite me to lunch or to a movie that will allow my mind to be free from thinking about my child for a few hours. Encourage me to exercise and get out of the house. I will eventually go, because I will eventually feel better. Don't give up on me and don't forget me. I am trying to do the best I can right now.

- **I MAY CRY AT TIMES IN FRONT OF YOU.** Please don't be embarrassed, and I won't be either. Besides being a natural emotion, crying is also a cleansing emotion. By crying, I can relieve a lot of anger, frustration, guilt and stress. Best of all, I feel much better after a good cry.

- **I PUT A MASK ON FOR THE PUBLIC.** Don't assume just because I am functioning during the day that I am "over it." I will never get "over it." I try to function normally because I have no other choice. You should see me when the day is over, and I am in the privacy of my own home and free to let my emotions out. My day mask comes off, and I am just a mother, aching for her child.

- **SOME DAYS MAY BE OVERWHELMING.** The slightest thing can trigger a bad time. It can be a song, a place I go, a holiday, a wedding or even smells or sounds. If I break down and start crying or seem to be in another world, it is because I am thinking of my child and longing for what I will never have again.

- **LET ME DO WHATEVER MAKES ME HAPPY.** Don't think me strange if I want to go to the cemetery a lot, if I want to buy a brick in honor of my child in every new building in town, or if I want to try to get new laws passed to keep this world safe for our children. I may need to try different things before I find what will be right for me in my new life. Encourage me to reach for the stars.

- **ACKNOWLEDGE MY GRIEF.** Don't ignore me because you are uncomfortable with the subject of death. It makes me wonder if what happened means nothing to you.

- **ANNIVERSARIES OF MY CHILD'S DEATH MAY BE PARTICULARLY DIFFICULT.** Perhaps if you could call or invite me out, it might help a little. At least acknowledge you also remember those important dates.

- **DON'T CALL WITH THE EXCUSE THAT YOU'VE BEEN TOO BUSY TO CALL.** Am I or my child that unimportant to you that you couldn't spare five extra minutes? I believe people make time for everything they think is important, and I appreciate those who just call and chat.

- **BECAUSE I HAVE SURVIVING CHILDREN DOESN'T MEAN THE PAIN OF LOSING A CHILD IS ANY EASIER.** The excruciating pain will always be there, whether an only child or one of many.

- **DON'T FORGET THE OTHER SPOUSE.** There are usually are two of us who have lost a child. Express your sympathy to both of us, not just me. My spouse hurts just as badly as I do, and his pain is as real as mine.

- **IF I HAVE SURVIVING CHILDREN ASK THEM HOW THEY ARE DOING** and encourage them to talk about their feelings also. Losing a sibling is just as devastating to them as losing a child is to me.

- **IF I ACT RUDE OR UNCARING AT TIMES, PLEASE FORGIVE ME.** The intense pain I feel is overriding any other emotions right then, and I truly don't mean to act that way.

- **LEAVE YOUR RELIGIOUS BELIEFS AT HOME.** I will cope with the religious aspect of my grief in my own way. What you believe may be much different from what I believe, so don't try to tell me things like, "It was God's will," or "Don't worry, you'll see your child again when you go to heaven."

- **BE AROUND FOR ME IF I NEED ANYTHING AND CAN'T SEEM TO GET IT DONE.** It could be just changing a light bulb, cleaning the house or shopping for food. There will be times I can't move and other times I feel exhausted. Try to understand these times.

- **ENCOURAGE ME TO START A NEW PROJECT,** join a new organization, or volunteer at someplace that could use my expertise. Perhaps a new job or new environment could help me. Talk to me about it.

I believe that if others can just do these things for us, our grief journey will become easier. I often think of this famous quote by Henri Houwen when I acknowledge who is a real friend. *"When we honestly ask ourselves which persons in our lives mean the most to us, we often find it is those who, instead of giving advice, cures or solutions, have chosen rather to share our pain and touch our wounds with a warm and tender hand. The friend who can be silent with us in a moment of despair and confusion, who can stay with us in an hour of grief and bereavement, who can tolerate not knowing, not healing, and face with us the reality of our powerlessness, that is a friend who cares."*

We will never forget our children. The pain never leaves. It just softens a little with time. We eventually function again, feel hope again, find joy in our lives. We travel a long road, but with the help of friends and relatives who understand a little of how we feel and what we are going through, perhaps that road will lead to new paths that enrich our lives in new ways we never dreamed were possible.

3. Commonalities Between Bereaved Parents

Commonalities exist between bereaved parents. When I was doing research for my first grief book, *I Have No Intention of Saying Good-bye,* I discovered after 25 interviews with bereaved parents the following five commonalities:

- **They want to leave memorials of some type to honor their child**
- **They choose to find a cause, a reason to move on with their lives and spoke of how they would live those lives**
- **They believe everyone grieves differently and at different rates, and that as painful as it is, it is important to go through this process to come to terms with the reality of the loss**
- **They know they will have setbacks and/or a rush of emotions that can be overwhelming when they might least expect it and that doesn't mean they will not heal**
- **They believe they are different people now than they were when their child was alive with different goals, different priorities, different friends, and a new life with a new richness to it that focuses on what our children left us...the gift of having them.**

The first commonality is ***they want to leave memorials of some type to honor their child.*** All parents want their child remembered and what better way to do that than to build memorials. These memorials can be anything from a scholarship named after them, to having their name on a newly built building, depending on your resources.

Some of the things I did were to start a journalism scholarship at my school so that every year I could tell Marcy's story to the audience at the senior honor's assembly before announcing the winner. Both my daughter and I were great fans of plays and any kind of theater production. Because of this, I bought bricks in newly constructed buildings in her memory and could say anything I wanted on the bricks (the building owners sold these bricks to raise money, and I was more than willing to oblige them). I did this at theaters, cultural centers and even the Diamondback Baseball Stadium. Her boss had a memorial area built at the Dorothy Chandler Pavilion in Los Angeles in her honor. When I attend a production, visit Los Angeles or go to a baseball game, I pause to look at them and smile. I know she is there smiling back at me for doing all these things in her memory. Even her best friend had a complete drama center built at a summer camp, collected the money and did the overseeing of the construction. A dedication at the end and a plaque placed on the building completed the project. Most recently, I started a foundation in her memory to benefit students and organizations related to communications and drama.

One mother in my book can now go to her church and see a painted mural of her two children along with other children who died. They are playing baseball in the mural, painted by a father who had also lost his son. Guided tours tell each child's story.

Another mother, invited to do a section of an AIDS quilt honoring her son who had died from the disease, got many of the son's friends to participate in the preparation of the section of quilt, and it made them all feel part of the memorial tribute. The display was in Drew University in New Jersey and in Washington, D.C. When the quilt is spread out, it stretches from the Capitol to the Washington Monument. San Francisco is now the home for the quilt and anyone can view it there.

Other parents find it important to speak to different groups about how their child died and relate the impact of the actions that caused the death. They do this in hopes of saving other lives in crisis. Some parents, like me, have written books to tell their story and offer advice that has helped others survive.

Still other parents choose to do their own quiet personal memorials at their home where they will celebrate birthdays and holiday or do activities in the schools the children attended. Many donate flowers to their church on the children's birthday or death day, while others decorate the children's graves at holidays such as Christmas.

There are so many things to help parents through their grief journey. Parents needs to decide what will work for them when they decide to honor and remember their children.

Choosing to find a cause, a reason to move on with your life is the second commonality. Parents may become very active in different organizations. These include Compassionate Friends, Bereaved Parents USA or Alive Alone for childless parents. Not only do they join these organizations to help themselves, but in time, they also start helping others who are just beginning the journey. Others who want to become even more involved get on the boards and help in any way they can to keep the organization vibrant for those who follow. Organizations such as Parents of Murdered Children or the Survivors of Suicide Victims have volunteers who help answer the phones. By becoming involved, you are not only helping the organization, you are helping yourself to grow and move on. For a list of many organizations, see the Resource section of this book.

One mother, whose daughter died at the hands of a drunk driver, became active in MADD where she can not only help others to become responsible drivers but also talk about her daughter and tell these people how much her daughter meant to her. Another mother whose daughter was also killed in a car accident now speaks to a Victims Impact Panel in the city where she lives, where part of the criminal's retribution is to listen to parent's stories and understand the loss. Becoming this involved helps some parents deal with their loss.

A father who lost a child started his own Compassionate Friends chapter in his hometown and found a new purpose to his life. New groups start all the time in a variety of cities dealing with infant loss, SIDS, stillbirths, cancer and other causes of death. All of these have a purpose: to help you, so you, in turn, can help others. When you are thinking of others and not only your own situation, you are moving forward.

Having a cause, a purpose in life, can be very rewarding. You will know when it is right for you and when everything will fall in place. Until then, keep working on what you want to do with the rest of your life, try to set a goal and aim to reach the sky.

The third commonality is ***everyone grieves differently and at different rates***. The first year, they say, is the worst. Some say it is the second year. Others say the third. No one is correct, because everyone has his or her own timelines. If one is to follow the five stages of grief: shock, anger, withdrawal, healing and renewal, some can do them in one year, others may take five years. Don't think that once you pass through a stage you are done with it. You can always go backwards before you go forward again. That is okay. It happens and it's nothing to be ashamed of or surprised about. The most important thing to remember is that everyone is different and no one grieves in a prescribed way.

Husbands and wives grieve differently and to hold your marriage together the best thing to do is to communicate with each other and if other children are involved, communicate with them. Talk about your child; remember the good times. Spouses should also talk about their fears. We become frighteningly insecure in grief and fear that everything we know and love will be swept away. Women tend to be more open with their feelings while men tend to hold everything back. Men believe they have to be the strong one in the family and so these bottled up feelings can come out in anger and at the wrong time, causing friction with the wife. If you think either of you need professional help, seek it, and don't wait until things get very bad. Remember, each spouse had a different relationship with the child; therefore, each experiences a different loss. One may be up emotionally while the other is down, or one may pass through one phase faster than the other may. Tempers are short and irritations flourish. Harsh things are said that aren't meant. A spouse could wrongly conclude that he or she can't depend on the partner for help in grieving.

To survive the heartaches of life, marriages must be built on trust. Nowhere is this more important than when we are plunged into the despair of parental grief.

When my daughter died I was no longer married to my daughter's father, so did not have that connection that many do. My husband at the time was Marcy's stepdad. Although we cried, talked and laughed about a Marcy story, in my heart I knew it was not the same loss for him as it was for me. He knew that, understood and even said so.

Everyone knows they will have setbacks and/or a rush of emotions that can be overwhelming, but that doesn't mean they won't heal is the fourth commonality. We have heard people say to us, "Isn't she over it yet? It's been a year since her child died." Yes, we have setbacks and probably always will when we hear our child's name, go to an event that our child used to participate in, or hear a song they once loved. We freeze and our mind returns to a day, a month or a year earlier before this happened. This is natural and others shouldn't look at it as though we are still where we were a year or so ago. We shouldn't look at it as though "we will never heal" from this. I think there is a difference between healing and just being able to move on. I almost don't like the word "heal." We never "heal" from the loss of a child. We continue to live, and in doing so, we accept what happened and try to make the best of it.

One mother told me, "One time I was asked to go to a soccer league game with a friend. I went, but had to leave in the middle. The overwhelming sensation that every time I looked at a player, my son's face intruded was just too much. It was over three years before I could attend another game comfortably."

It has been many years since Marcy died. This week I was looking through all the photo albums I've accumulated over my lifetime. Each album brought back memories of my childhood, Marcy growing up, and what I've done since she died. It was both a joy and painful to go through those albums, but I did find periods of time I thought were lost forever. Now I know I will always have them in pictures and be able to look at them. I cried during the process, remembering all I had and all those I have lost over the years, including the most precious of them all, my only child. I know that I will always cry going through these photos and any items I have from her life. Am I regressing? No, I'm not. It is all part of the healing process.

New friends say to me sometimes, "You are so amazing. I could never live through what you have lived through. I would just die." My answer to them is always, "What choice do we have when this happens to us? If we want to continue with our lives for our spouse, for our other children if we have them, or for ourselves, we will adjust to our present situation and deal with it. I have been able to do that as many others have. I don't like it. I'd do anything to have my daughter back here with me, but that is not going to happen and I know it. Therefore, we move on, but we keep our child in our heart forever. They will always be with us in whatever we do, in wherever we go, and that is comforting to me.

The final commonality is that ***after the death of a child, we change; we have different goals, different priorities, different friends and a new life***. My goals, which were once to make sure my daughter had a rich, full life, are no longer there. My reason for living, for doing what I did, is gone. It took a while to decide what I now wanted to do with my life, and I can say I have found the answer for myself. It is to help other bereaved parents, and I do that through my book, my blog, and my speaking engagements at bereavement conferences and elsewhere, where I can share my story and teach others to learn to accept what we can become without our child.

My priorities have also changed. What was once important to us may no longer have any meaning. What others talk about, like the economy or global warming is insignificant to us during our grief journey. We feel powerless over life after the loss of a child. It's hard to believe how much energy it takes just to go on.

Grief rewrites your address book for you. I lost good friends when Marcy died. They didn't want to be around me. They thought I had changed. Of course, I had changed. They also probably thought that what happened to me could happen to them; so they didn't want to hear me speak of it. The truth was, as I have found out in recent years, that a few of them were scared, they didn't know what to say or do for me. The easiest thing was for them to fade into the background. They didn't realize what they were doing hurt more than anything they could have said. Only someone who has been through this can truly understand and help, and I couldn't expect those few (some of whom have come back now) to understand what, at the time, was incomprehensible to me also.

People are funny about death. Until the 1980's it was a hush, hush topic. Death wasn't spoken about in a home, especially if it was a child's death. There were no books, no organizations to help bereaved parents. Shoving your grief under the bed was the order of the day. Thank goodness, by the 1990's there was help out there in the form of books and newly formed grief organizations. There will always be those who still feel that way about death; they do not want to talk about it to you and "it didn't happen."

On the other hand, I discovered that people who were just acquaintances became better friends than those I thought were good friends. I appreciated them for being empathetic to my situation and wanting to listen to what I had to say. I am sure many of you have had the same experience. I now have new friends who talk about Marcy and allow me to do the same. The following saying comforts me: "A friend is one who knows you as you are, understands where you've been, accepts who you've become, and still gently invites you to grow."

Finally, an apropos quote I invite you all to follow that I use in one of my speeches and needs no explanation: "Life isn't about waiting for the storm to pass; it's about learning to dance in the rain." Go dance your heart out!

4. *Preserving a Child's Memory*

The most important thing to parents after the death of a child is keeping that child's memory in the minds and hearts of others. They don't want to forget their child, nor do they want others to forget. They want people to talk about the child, say their name and tell of an event related to the child...anything that will keep the memory alive. I have summed up briefly here what I may mention in other articles but its importance cannot be denied. Use these ideas and others to preserve your child's memory.

Parents can do many things to honor their child. Many parents set up **scholarship funds** in memory of the child at the school he or she attended. Each year a winner of the scholarship is chosen, and some parents like to do the actual presentation so they can say a little bit about their child in the process.

A good memory is having a 20-inch **Carrie Bear** made from a piece of favorite clothing belonging to your child and displayed on a bed. It helps another person feel close to someone who is lost. Go to www.carriebears@juno.com and see an assortment of bears and the way they are made. A photo of your child can also be included on the bear.

Journaling one's feelings after your child dies is a way to look back and see how you were feeling during those awful first few months or years. Releasing those pent up feelings is good for you, and crying is very healthy, so don't be ashamed. Most importantly, journaling shows how far you have come.

A web site of the child has become very popular. Parents can tell all about him or her, scan in pictures and even play music. Although I don't have a web site, I do have a video a friend made of my daughter that I enjoy showing to both old friends and new friends. I enjoy sharing her life and personality with them, and they appreciate getting to know my daughter more intimately.

A great gift a parent can receive is to have a **newborn named after the child**. I was fortunate to have my daughter's best friend name her first daughter after mine. At first, I thought I might feel awkward saying her name, but I don't. She is not my daughter, but carries with her a story of a very wonderful person. She now understands who she is named after and has asked me what happened. I happily talk about my daughter, and once more, my daughter is not forgotten.

I took a color (or you can use black and white) picture of my daughter to a J.C. Penney's store jewelry department (other stores may do it also). I chose a gold oval **pendant** (I liked the oval best but there are also round, square and heart-shaped ones), and then the store sends it to a company that embosses the picture directly onto the gold pendant. It takes approximately six weeks. I don't know the process, but the results are beautiful. It is something I always wear to keep my daughter close to my heart. People do notice and comment on how nice it looks. Those who don't know me ask who it is; others ask, "Is it you?" I smile. I guess Marcy did look a little like me. I then have a chance to talk about her to others.

When I hear about a child dying, whether I knew that child or not, I have on occasion **sent letters or cards** to those grieving parents. I start by saying that I am sorry for their loss. I tell them my story as a qualifier for writing to them and it gives me one more opportunity to talk about Marcy. I give suggestions of what organizations they can contact or grief groups they can join to help them through the difficult times. I tell them surviving grief is a lifelong process, one they will have to go through, but eventually, they will move forward with their lives and find joy again. I feel good writing these parents and find it helps me in my journey also.

I have put together a **photo/music presentation** of my daughter from her birth picture through her last days. I tried to choose ones where her personality clearly showed through. The instrumental music chosen was upbeat and light. I have it on my computer and can go to it whenever I feel her presence and need more of her. I also have a DVD copy of the pictures to show friends who knew her and even those who didn't know her. I also find that because I do talk about her, it is important for my special friends to see and hear her on tape. Fortunately, a friend of hers, a videographer, put together for me a 15-minute tape of her life, as he knew her in her adult years. She radiates throughout the tape as a fun-loving, beautiful soul. There is never a dry eye in the room after people have viewed the video.

Along the same lines, I saved all of Marcy's annual **school photos** and took a large frame, dividing it into 16 wallet size spaces and placed a picture from birth to 16 years in it. Not only is it a wonderful conversation piece when I am showing people around my home, but it is also a wonderful representation of how much a child changes in 16 years! Other projects you can do with photos are a collage in time segments; for example, age 1-5, 6-10, 11-15, etc. and place them side by side on a wall. I have done both. For those who like to walk into a room and see your child's smiling face, place a framed photo in each room. For those who think this is too much, pick a prominent spot where friends and guests coming to your home will see the photo. This may produce conversations about your child that might have otherwise gone unsaid.

When I speak at national bereavement conferences, I can tell **Marcy stories** and feel comfortable knowing I am in a safe environment where parents want to hear other's stories because only *they* truly understand. I speak at university grief classes held during the year, at local bereavement groups, and at organizations that want to know more about how to relate to bereaved parents.

When I have to give a birthday or anniversary gift to a friend (particularly one who has everything imaginable), or I go to a luncheon and need a gift, I **donate money** to my favorite charity, the endowment fund I recently set up in Marcy's memory! In that way, people learn about the fund and about Marcy. I have given them something worthwhile to think about donating to, since it is for students who need monetary help to pursue their careers in communications or theater. This fund will be around long after I am gone, and I hope others will continue to support it.

In each case, I come away with a good feeling that on any particular day I am able to share my Marcy with the world and keep her memory alive.

5.   Recognizing Guilt and Dealing With It

*If I hadn't worked throughout my pregnancy…If I had taken her to the doctor when she complained of that stomach ache…If I hadn't let him use the car that night…If I had only noticed the change in him, perhaps I could have kept him from suicide…*All of these laments are statements many of us have heard or even said ourselves. All the "what if's" will not bring our children back, but the guilt that the children are gone lingers. Common types of guilt follow and some suggestions of what you can do to help yourself cope.

Regrets

As parents, we believe we are responsible for our children's well-being. If something happens to them…an accident, an illness, a drug related problem or more…we feel guilty and that it is our fault. We feel helpless. We should have been able to prevent it. We should have taken better care of our child. We should have been able to save our child. These are thoughts that run through our heads.

One mother in my last book had to deal with the death of her child when she sent him to a therapy camp for drug users and he died there when he became ill and no one believed him. Living with how he died is still the greatest challenge of her life. She believes she sent him to his death. Her guilt feelings have tortured her for many years. "I am his mother," she said. "Intellectually, I know I'm not responsible for his death, but meshing my intellect with my heart is very difficult. I will probably struggle with this for the rest of my life." She tried to help the son she loved so much, yet the results were only disaster and

22

continual guilt she lives with to this day. She realizes that if she lets it, the guilt could consume her. Instead, she knows her intentions were good and she must try to live her life for the other members of her family. This mother understands that feeling less guilty won't take away the anger, pain or sadness, but that it is worth the effort to take a realistic look at forgiving yourself.

Guilt With or Without Foundation

Parents often feel they are punished for something they have done if their child dies, even if they have done nothing wrong. When we get angry with our child or aren't speaking to them because they did something wrong in our eyes, we feel tremendous guilt if that child dies before we can reconcile with them. This becomes a form of self-torture.

When we outlive our child, we have survivor's guilt. A parent may ask, "Why am I alive and my child died? We were in the same car crash. My child had so much potential, so much to live for." One mother told me she would have done anything to save her child, donate an organ, a limb…anything, even if it meant her own death.

We may not be able to get through this by ourselves. We need the help of others who understand and can be more objective than we are. To rid ourselves of guilt we must accept the fact that we are human. We get mad at our kids, and we love our kids. No relationship is perfect.

If parents work long hours and can't spend a lot of time with the kids, guilt enters the picture if a child dies, and they feel they have been punished for working too much and not paying enough attention to the child. For some, this type of guilt can be instrumental in spending time that is more creative with the remaining children. For others, nothing changes and the guilt remains.

When grieving, we may be acting strangely or differently, leading to guilty feelings that we are not normal. For example, crying for seemingly no reason or getting out of town when others think you should be at home mourning, are perfectly normal reactions for someone who is grief stricken. Do what is right for you, not what you think others expect you to do and don't feel guilty about it.

Guilt Resulting in Relief

If you have a child with a long-term illness or disability, when death occurs, you may feel you have already done your mourning before the death happened. If the child was in severe pain, then death may come as a relief. This relief may be mingled with guilt over the fact that you are glad to be relieved of the burden. There may be guilt that you are glad they are no longer in pain or suffering, or guilt that you are still alive and they are gone.

It takes courage to admit you are not perfect and telling it like it is seems to be the best way to deal with this. Share your guilt feelings with supportive, caring people, a grief group and if necessary, professional counseling. Do not let it fester and become destructive to you and others. Let the love you feel for your child shine through any guilt feelings.

6.   *Now Childless Issues*

When a parent loses an only child or all their children, we learn there are unique aspects that confront us because we are now childless.

QUESTIONS PARENTS MAY ASK

- **Am I still a mother/father?**
- **Do I need to make a new will?**
- **Will there be any special events in my life?**
- **Do I have to listen to others talk about their children and grandchildren?**
- **Will my marriage be affected?**
- **Will I lose friends who still have children?**
- **Will others understand the new me?**

First, ***Am I still a mother/father****?* Of course we are. We will always be a parent, whether our child is alive or dead, and we should think of ourselves in that way, no matter who may ask.

It does become awkward when someone we first meet asks us if we have any children. How should we answer that question? Please don't ever say, "None." Acknowledge that at one time there was a child or many children. By saying, "None" we are saying they never existed. For me, I just simply say, "I have one daughter who died in a car accident. She was 27 at the time." Although the other person may now feel awkward, didn't we, too, feel awkward when confronted with the question? Tell it like it is and go from there. Acknowledging we are mothers/fathers and will always be parents will make all of us feel better, and now we can ask the other person the same question and release the tension, letting them talk about their children. We have said what we needed to, and everyone is more comfortable about it.

Second, ***Do I need to make a new will?*** The answer is, "Yes, you probably do." If your child was not married and did not have any children from that marriage, you need to think about your will, your trust and any legal issues that will entail. To whom do you leave your money and possessions? If you have a grandchild, the task may be easier. Many of us who don't have grandchildren may have siblings, aunts, uncles, cousins, and special friends who are possibilities. There is always a charity happy to take a donation. I do not have any siblings or blood relatives, but I do have three Godchildren from my daughter's best friend. They are now in my will, as are some friends, some of my favorite charities and a foundation to honor my daughter. I am very specific as to who gets what and just have to make sure that my wishes are followed. That is the best for which I can hope.

Third, ***Will there be any special events in my life?*** Not as far as going to your child's graduation, birthday parties, wedding or birth of a grandchild, for example. When our friends have these happy occasions and talk about them, they tear at our hearts. When my friend's son got married a few months after my daughter died, I couldn't go to the wedding. I explained why to her and she understood. Years later, it became easier, but I still think of my daughter and all that she is missing. I go to events, smile and congratulate where appropriate, but it is a sad time. My daughter should be here attending these events in my place or with me. It will never be, and I must accept that.

Fourth, ***Do I have to listen to others talk about their children and grandchildren?*** My bridge friends talk about their children and grandchildren all the time. They have every right to talk about them, but they should also understand how I feel when they go on and on about them. Unless they have lived through a child's death, they can never understand what I am going through. I hide it pretty well, but if given the opportunity to say something about my daughter Marcy, I'll certainly take that opportunity, whether they want to hear or not. They may be thinking, "Why is she talking about her dead child?" Why do you think? My daughter was all I had, and I will always have her as far as I'm concerned. What better way to keep her memory alive than to talk about her. She is as important to me as my friend's children are to them. What I find so wonderful is when someone says to me, "And how did Marcy react to that in high school or college?" allowing me to gladly join in with a story.

Fifth, **Will my marriage be affected?** If you had a good relationship with your spouse to begin with, chances are that the death of your only child will not hurt your marriage. If the reason you were together, though, was only the child, there is a good chance your marriage may be in trouble. Despite what many people think, if a marriage breaks up, it is not because of the child's death but because there was something wrong with the marriage in the first place. If your marriage is worth saving in your eyes, seek help during this awful time in your life. Another problem could relate to "significant others." Are they supportive? Do they understand what you are going through? Do they let you talk and express pent up feelings? Does your grief and loss cause problems in the relationship with not only the significant other but with any stepchildren? I am very lucky that my husband has a wonderful daughter who I am very close to. She reminds me a lot of my daughter. Their personalities are similar; they are both spirited with minds of their own; their birthdays are identical except for the year born. She gets along with her parents as Marcy did with her dad and me. Others are not quite as fortunate, and I would again encourage those who need professional help to get it and not wait until it's too late.

Sixth, **Will I lose friends who still have children?** Many newly bereaved parents believe their friends are uncomfortable around them now. They are probably right! They are uncomfortable because they don't know what to say, they think we've changed or they simply feel they don't want what happened to me to rub off on them. When Marcy died, good friends who I thought would be there for me were not. Others who hardly knew Marcy camped at my doorstep. I was so surprised at how people reacted, and I hear others also talk about it all the time. I found that I made new friends, friends that have brought new meaning to my life and try very hard to understand the new me. "Grief shoves away friends and scares away so-called friends and rewrites your address book for you." Oh, that is so true.

Lastly, ***Will others understand the new me?*** I am a different person from what I was when my daughter was alive. I have new goals and new priorities. What was once important to me may no longer have any meaning. I ask for patience as I go through my grief journey. I ask for understanding that there is no set time limit to my grief. Grief makes what others think of us moot. It shears away the masks of normal life and forces brutal honesty out of your mouth before propriety can stop you. Don't cry over a broken plate. Don't worry about gas going up five cents this week. Those things are insignificant and no longer important after our child dies. We feel powerlessness over life after the loss of a child. It's hard to believe how much energy it takes just to go on. We've been slammed against a brick wall, and the slamming comes again and again. We are suffering through the most unbearable loss of all, but we are all survivors. We will never forget, we will never get over it, but we *will* eventually move on with our lives. What other choice do we have?

7. *How Those in Mourning Show Their Grief*

When we are in the very depths of grieving over the death of our child, we may react in various ways. We may show our grief openly to others, we may hide our grief and never speak of it, we may refuse to adapt or we try to adapt to our new life. Those going through the grief journey should be aware of these reactions and seek professional help where necessary.

Showing grief openly

Our precious child is gone. We mourn; we cry; we want others to know how we are feeling. We find it difficult to function, to do everyday chores, even to get out of bed in the morning.

One bereaved father could not go to work in the morning for a very long time. His grief had paralyzed him. He didn't want to go anywhere or do anything. When friends came over, all he did was cry and talk about his child. When friends wanted to take him out, he refused. He sat at home, staring at pictures of his child, and asked the eternal question, "Why?" Friends began to drift away after many calls and no response. Only through the help of a professional counselor did he begin to function again and was able to move on, call people, go out, enjoy life. He started his journey by making a very short list of what he was going to do when he got out of bed that day. His list at first consisted of only taking a shower and making breakfast. That was all he could manage. When he was able to do that, he added another chore to his list (make the bed) and then another (drive around the block), until his list became long enough that he was able to add "go to work." At work, it was another struggle to wipe his mind clear and think about his job and what needed to be done. Co-workers noticed and were patient. It was a very slow process, but eventually this parent survived. He has little recollection of some of his responses, but he credits his co-workers with the ability to help him while under pressure to get their own work done. "I was a mess, but they empathized; they were compassionate," he said. "That was all I could ask for at the time."

Hiding grief

It didn't happen. We don't want anyone to talk about our dead child. It is like putting all thoughts of the child under the bed and out of sight. The clothes go; the toys go; the pictures are put away. We don't want people to see us mourn, and if asked how we are, we answer, "I'm doing fine."

However, are we 'fine?' Some bereaved parents might think so. They might think they have moved on and they continue with their lives as though nothing has happened.

One parent had a friend who had been very close to the child. Each time she brought up the child's name, the parent gave her friend "the look." That look said, "Who asked you to mention my child, my child is dead, there is no reason to discuss it, and the hurt is too painful." Moreover, therein lay the crux of the problem. This parent loved her child very much; there was no denying that. Losing the child was simply too painful to discuss and to think about. She denied any feelings or emotions and truly believed the sensible thing to do would be to hide her feelings.

One family counselor believes this denial of any emotions is definitely not good for you and can lead to problems in your marriage, your job, your relationship with other family members and your relationship with friends. Talking about your feelings is a better solution. If not a counselor, then choose someone you can trust completely.

Not adapting

I am aware of a friend's daughter who lost a child and for the past seven years, she has been a bitter, moody person. She sees no reason that this should have happened to her. She has yet to make sense of any of it. She is a woman who is mad at life and what life has done to her. She treats her family indifferently, not wanting to go anywhere with them or do anything with or for them. Her husband does most of the cooking now. Her other children are lacking the all-important attention they need from her. She doesn't realize they are all mourning the sibling loss also. She sits at home and mourns her loss; she has become selfish in that she sees no further than this loss being her private loss; she has made no effort to get help, nor does she find that reading books on grief are doing any good (she starts but doesn't finish them).

Going by herself, sometimes she visits her mom in another state. Her mom sees what she is doing to herself, but feels she cannot help her daughter. She even asked me to talk to her, and I could see the bitterness show through clearly. I made a few suggestions. One was to go to a grief group like Compassionate Friends (there are over 600 chapters in the U.S.) where she will discover others feel as she does and hopefully, as they all talk, get help from those who have been there and now can cope. I also suggested she needed to get more involved with the rest of her family and talk to them about their feelings, wants and needs. If she doesn't do that at least, the entire family could go on a downward spiral and hopefully, she wouldn't want that to happen. A grief counselor, and only one who has also lost a child and understands what she is going through, can be a great help.

Grief is very hard work and you must work through it in whatever way is easiest and most appropriate for you. Part of this work is accepting the finality of loss, which this woman has yet to do.

Adapting

We must go through a specific grief process to come out on the other side. It is a difficult, scary journey but necessary. Allowing yourself to feel the pain will help you get through it. Those of us who have accepted the death of our child have gone through the shock, anger, withdrawal, healing and renewal. Each one of these phases can take a long or short time, depending on the person. You may discover that you will even come back to some of them repeatedly, but you know you want to do something useful with your life and so you plough on.

What I, personally, decided to do with my life was many-fold. I wanted to preserve my daughter's memory and do this in many ways. I buy memorials at different locations, whether it is a brick or a new building with her name on it. I travel as she loved to do and always wear my Marcy necklace and feel she is with me all the time. I talk about her to anyone who will listen, when appropriate to the conversation. I find that helping others through my writings also helps me. I became a more compassionate person and find my desire to help others has increased tremendously over the years. I have a full life now with my husband and stepdaughter (who happens to be born on Marcy's birthday and is so like her. Coincidence? Who knows what strange things God has planned for us in our new life.) Through it all, I never, never stop thinking of my daughter and never will. I smile at the good memories and know she is looking down at me and smiling.

Death makes us examine our lives and reevaluate who we are and who we want to become in our new lives. When we find those answers, we will have gone through our pain, faced it, and accepted it as best we can.

8. The Grief Journey: What You Know; What the Future Holds

The grief journey after losing a child is the hardest journey a person will ever take. Here are a few ideas for you to ponder.

What you now know about grief:

- You have lost the most important person in your life.
- Breaking down physically, mentally and emotionally from the entire trauma you have gone through is possible.
- You become a different person.
- It is important to take care of yourself to stay healthy and well.
- You find yourself crying all the time.
- Losing old friends is inevitable.
- Everything becomes a blurred memory and you are not quite sure how to handle it.
- It is so overwhelming.
- You know you must go on and do not really want to.
- People do not understand your anxiety and find it difficult to help you.
- You can fall apart any minute of any day.
- At this point, you do not really care about anything or anyone except the child you lost.
- Making any kind of decision is difficult.
- You cannot sleep at night.

What you will find in your future:

- You have become a better, more caring person.
- You will rewrite your address book.
- New friends will accept who you are and who you will become.
- People who are going through the same experience can be of comfort.
- A deeper appreciation of others, particularly family members will be in your thoughts.
- Being a more compassionate person is your goal.
- Strength you never knew you had begins to show.
- You have faced the worst thing that could happen and survived.

Remember, "Grief is not about getting over it. It's about coming through it and finding a way to deal with it by moving forward with your life."

9. I'm Doing the Best I Can

When we are on a grief journey and someone asks us, "How are you feeling?" the tendency is to say, "I'm fine." However, we are not fine, and one of my friends said that to me a few months after my daughter died. She said in a rather exasperated voice, "You're not fine, and don't say you are!" I was briefly stunned and then realized she was right. Why say you are 'fine' when you are not. What it taught me is that from that point on, I told the truth. My answer became, "I'm doing the best I can. Each day is a challenge, and I try to get through it intact."

What a relief it was to tell it like it was! According to author and grief counselor, Dr. Lou La Grand, in an online Ezine article he wrote, "Grief is a normal human response due to the death of a loved one. If you try to pretend you are doing well when you are not, you will guarantee that the pain will spill out in unexpected ways. You may prolong the intensity of your grief process and add unnecessary suffering to legitimate pain and sadness."

Here are some ideas for you to follow so you don't have to pretend you are doing well.

- Admit you are hurting. It is usually obvious to most people, even the ones who are not skilled professionals.
- Cry for as long as you want and no matter who is listening or watching. By crying, you relieve pent up emotions and feel much better. Cry with people you want to be around like relatives, friends or even during a grief group session. Those in a grief group understand your reason for crying and may be able to cry with you and comfort you. Don't

be embarrassed when you cry. You have every right to grieve in any way that helps you.

- Sometimes it is a good idea to be by yourself and reflect on what has happened to you. This does not mean you should go off by yourself and do things alone all the time. Don't become isolated. You need to be around others to seek their advice and help.
- Read about other people's grief journey who are convinced they had a sign or message from a deceased loved one. Explore the possibility. Many do believe in life after death. At a recent Compassionate Friends National Conference where I spoke, I was fortunate to hear another speaker whose son died. He showed us proof of the fact that we get signs from our children who have left us that they will always be around for us.
- Grieve at your own pace. You may need less time than others or more time. Both are normal. When we choose to love, we automatically choose to grieve. Although the person is no longer physically present, love never dies; it lives on forever.

Your loved one lives on through you. The history of loss shows you will survive and move on with your life.

10. One View on Using a Recovery Program

Not everyone agrees that a grief support group is what all bereaved parents need. One psychology counselor, speaker and author Dr. Maurice Turmel says in an Ezine article on the web about using a recovery program that support groups are just that; they offer support but no direction. He believes that these parents are simply recycling their pain and not moving forward with their recovery. He believes parents should go through a "proper recovery program" and incorporate a support group within the recovery program, if they chose to do so.

In the end, he says, it does not matter what took your child from you. The grieving and healing process you must undergo remains the same. Dealing with feelings through therapy, group work and guided journaling are the tools and practices necessary for recovery. He successfully uses this approach for all his grieving clients. "Everyone who pursued this program completed their recovery and got on with their lives," he said.

"There is no substitute for working through your grief if you truly want to heal," he adds. "Some people simply refuse to move forward, hanging on to their grief as if they were hanging on to their child. They don't accept that they can actually heal and hold on to that precious child in a loving and expansive way rather than continue with their suffering."

He continued, "You have to choose healing in order to recover from grief. You have to commit to your own recovery just like any other person who is stuck in some disabling condition. And those wonderful memories you had of each other before the tragedy, where do they go if you choose suffering?"

I have a friend whose husband cannot get past the last two weeks of his son's life in the hospital. He cannot remember the good times because of it. He is stuck. I can see where this type of program would help him tremendously. On the other hand, there are those who only go to grief groups and find that is enough for them to move on. For myself, I read every book I could get my hands on and that is what helped me. I could identify with different feelings and situations when reading, and I began to understand that my feelings were normal, and I had to help myself climb out of the abyss and into the sunlight again.

I think this program suggested by Dr. Turmel would be excellent for those who are stuck and for those who need a helping hand to see where they are and where they are going.

11. Women and How They Grieve

Women throughout their lives are encouraged to express feelings. It is okay for young girls to become emotional and cry about losing a part in the school play or missing an "A" on an exam by one point. As they get older, they routinely take care of their siblings, dry dishes or even clean the house. They are being prepared for a nurturing role, and they take it seriously.

When a woman has a child, that nurturing role begins to take effect. She cares for the child, feeds them, and keeps them safe from all harm. A beautiful relationship forms, and the love flows freely between them. If that child dies, her whole world shatters. Suddenly this role as mother is torn from her and she responds accordingly. Tears, screaming, recriminations, and the thought that she, in any way, caused this situation she now finds herself in leaves her emotionally drained and fearful. She agonizes over the fact that no lunches need making, no parks need visiting, no school happenings to attend and no long talks between the two of them. In short, her life has changed completely.

In some cases, the father is right there to help, in other cases, not so. Fathers are taught to be strong, not to show emotions, and certainly not to cry. The mother is often offended that the father is not there for her and her needs. He is off ranting and raving to friends, to doctors and to anyone who will listen to him about his loss. Marriage problems could ensue until the couple tries to get help.

There is no perfect way to grieve, but through therapy, the mother may be able to release her anger and frustration at not being able to change this outcome and learn that others in the family need her nurturing now, including her husband.

Suggestions for bereaved mothers:

- Acknowledge any anxiety you have during your grief period. If you do, it will eventually leave. Don't run from it, face it.
- You are physically and mentally exhausted from all the emotions that have welled up during your initial grief period. Get more rest during the day and go to bed earlier at night. You will be more alert and able to face the day.
- Use good friends for support and be able to talk to them about your child. They can help you remember good times and loving thoughts. Share your feelings with them.
- Enjoy the small pleasures as best as possible during this time. Be kind to yourself.
- Spend time alone to clear your mind. Perhaps a short day or overnight trip will help you not to think negatively. Taking time for *you* is important.
- Do not expect too much from others in the family or from yourself at this time. Don't assume you and your husband will be in the same place or moving at the same pace through the grief process. However, you must be on the same page as your husband with total honesty and trust between the two of you.
- There is no perfect way to deal with your grief. Do what you feel is right for you, whether it is positive or negative.
- Read a book by a bereaved mother who pours out her heart and soul to you. My suggestions include *Beyond Tears* by Ellen Mitchel, *Comfort* and *The Knitting Circle* by Ann Hood, *First You Die* by Marie Levine, *Love Never Dies* by Sandy Goodman, *My Teen Angel* by Sally Silagy, and *Star Child* by Jennifer Martin.

12. Dealing with Anger When Grieving

When I lost my daughter, the anger surfaced immediately. "What a waste of a beautiful life, what a waste that she should have died," I kept saying to myself. Those two words, "a waste" continually ran through my mind. She had so much to live for, so much to do, so much to accomplish. In a split second, it was all gone. Twenty-seven years of nurturing, loving, and being so proud of the person I had brought into this world.

The driver of the van who hit her car was gone in a second, running and running, never found. Friends asked, "Aren't you mad he was never found, so he could be punished?" I thought hard about that answer and finally determined, "No, I didn't want to have to sit in a courtroom and hear the rehash of what happened and have to look him in the eye and remember his face always. I was much better off emotionally not having to go through that and have any more recurring nightmares than I already had."

Sure, it would be justice to see him punished, but was it worth all the other emotions it would conjure up. He knew what he did; he had to live with that the rest of his life. With that type of person who would run from the scene of an accident, my mind said that he would probably do it again someday and maybe next time get caught. A friend once said to me, "Everyone eventually gets their just rewards." It is probably true, but at that time, it did not matter. He had already done the worst possible thing one human could do to another…he killed the most important person in my life. Nothing else mattered.

My anger was directed at how meaningless this death was, how it should never have happened.

One psychologist said that anger is a unique subjective experience. For most of us, it generates changes in physical sensations, including increased heart rate and muscle tension, shallow breathing and disruptions in sleep and appetite. For others, anger promotes feelings of guilt, shame, self-loathing and even depression. Anger can create errors in reasoning or judgment, poor concentration, and strong feelings of helplessness.

On the other hand, anger may become the motivating force for noble and valuable action; for example, taking action against a wrong that needs to be righted, a law that needs to be changed or a community that needs to see that what they are doing can do more harm than good. One may work as a volunteer with MADD, Victim Impact groups or similar organizations that try to correct many situations. This reaction can be both healing and helpful at the same time.

In the case of a grieving parent, anger is natural. We may not consciously acknowledge our anger, but it is usually there to some degree. This is especially true for women, who are discouraged from showing anger and trained to be "nice." Because females have been nurturers and peacemakers, when they express anger, they are considered "controlling" or "bossy." Women fear anger because others disapprove, and women think it would make matters worse. So they tend to hold anger in, which can bring other physical complications.

Men are raised to be more aggressive, so when faced with frustration or helplessness, such as when their child dies, they tend to respond differently from women and get angrier, sometimes taking out the death on someone else, yelling and going a bit crazy. They may even try to sue everyone in sight for the child's death, losing all perspective. Anger is available, and it allows them to release all the pent up shock to their system. Men's rage eventually moves into the third phase of grief, a quieter place that allows rest and dealing with feelings in a more appropriate way. Like the grief journey itself, it may take a short or long period to reach that level, but eventually they will find themselves there and not even realize what has happened in the interim.

Catherine Sanders, in her book *Surviving Grief and Learning to Live Again* listed some sources of anger that cause discomfort when grieving and one that does not. They include:

- **confrontive anger**, when we don't get the support or encouragement we expect or need from family and friends and become irritable or hostile towards them
- **displaced anger**, when we blame someone for this tragedy because they are available
- **internalized anger**, when we turn it inward causing physical problems, depression and hopelessness
- **helpless anger**, when we are powerless and not in control and tend to cry and have outbursts
- **appropriate anger**, a very healthy type of anger, when we can openly discuss why we are angry or vent our anger alone or with a special friend, get it all out and feel relieved.

"Anger is a difficult emotion to express in bereavement, because we feel that we are under the close scrutiny of others, said Ms. Sanders. "We want to do things correctly and set a good example. However, our own needs should be our top priority. When we take care of ourselves, we set the best example of all."

13. Strategies for Dealing With Pain and Suffering

A powerful Buddhist quote: "Pain is inevitable, suffering is optional." When we are in pain, our heart aches and our body feels numb, because someone we love is gone. When we suffer, we may ask, "Will we ever be able to move on? We are in a rut. We resist getting better."

The onslaught of pain is inevitable when a child dies. This human being was part of us. We helped make this person, so naturally, if they die (for whatever reason), a part of us dies also, and our heart breaks. Shock, anger, fright and shaken: any of these emotions can cause pain. It may take either a short or a long while before our pain is gone, but some never move on or accept what happened. These people are suffering unnecessarily. Some strategies might help those who are having difficulty moving forward and beyond suffering.

- Write a journal about your feelings. If you have a bad dream or even a good dream, write it down in the morning and reflect on it later in the day.
- Take a long walk each day to reflect, cry, pray or just sit by yourself.
- Describe your feelings in a poem, drawing or letter to your loved one and put away for a while, look at it again and reflect on what you said or sketched.
- See a grief counselor or spiritual leader. These people often have words of wisdom to guide you along on your

journey and no one else needs to know you have seen them, if you find it embarrassing.

- Do things with family. Although this may bring back memories you want to forget, it may also bring back good memories of your loved one that you can keep in your heart forever and think about often.
- Ask friends to share memories of your loved one. Hard as you may try, you can't remember everything, and your friends may be able to lighten your heart and mind with a story that you can treasure forever.
- To feel connected to your loved one, wear a piece of clothing or piece of jewelry that was once theirs.
- Do a small pamphlet of your loved one's life in pictures and words, and give it to special family and friends who you believe never want your loved one forgotten.
- Contribute to a cause or start a scholarship fund or foundation in memory of your loved one. See that others can make their lives better through your help. Your loved one would be proud of you.
- Be a friend to another person who is grieving. Shared experiences can help both of you going through the grieving process.
- Live each day to the fullest. Help others when needed. Hug others when they need your touch. Show patience, sympathy, and empathy to others. Give others what you would also like to have, a soft touch, an understanding smile, a shoulder to lean on, and it will come back to you ten-fold.

We must make a commitment to ourselves that we will do the best we can in the midst of our loss, and our life will have more meaning and reach a realistic fulfillment. Follow your heart by taking one step at a time to deal with your pain and suffering.

14. *Time and Its Function When Grieving*

I was talking, recently, to a friend whose husband suddenly died last year. Coincidentally, another friend whose husband died years ago was standing with me. My friend asked how the other woman with the recent loss was doing. She answered, "Very well, thanks."

I looked at her and thought, yes, she does look much better, as I knew she would after a year or longer. "Time is a great healer," said my other friend, and to me, "in most cases." I knew she was referring to the fact that the loss of a child was too great a loss for anyone to have to bear. I appreciated her comment, but became very teary-eyed, as I nodded my head and agreed with my friend. The passage of time will ease most pain. I got to thinking about time in relationship to grieving and realized time plays an important function in the grief process in general.

Time as a gift. In relationship to our child, the time we spent with them is priceless. As we think of them now that they are gone, time stops for us. We want to remember everything we said to them, all the activities we went to with them, all the loving moments of hugging and kissing. Some of us record what we can remember (and it won't be everything). We can then ask others what they remember and record some more. As the days, month, and years pass, we will continue to remember, as will others. Keep recording and you will discover the gift of remembrance and comfort.

Impatient with time. Time can be a negative in our grief journey. Can we do this grief journey? How long will it take? We are impatient. We want all this to be over with, and soon. It will not happen that way. Time will not release us. We do not like that our child is gone; we do not like that our spouse, our parents, our friends cannot make us feel better. We want to know what we can do to move us along this journey. Wanting to heal is a good sign. Just take it slowly and be patient.

Time and choices. In our grief, will we make wise choices? We tend to want others to make those choices for us, relieving us from that burden. We may not even care about what happens in our future right now. Do not feel that way. Take charge, whether we have the energy right now or not. Reclaim yourself.

Time to move on. As much as we would like to heal and get better quickly, that will not happen and others cannot expect us to be better in a month, a few months, or even a year. Everyone grieves differently and everyone is entitled to move at his or her own pace. Others may get impatient with us, may be uncomfortable with our need to talk about our loss, but that becomes their problem. They may walk away from us, but is that not their loss? We try to be the friend they want, but it is very hard. We hope they understand, but most do not. Now we need friends who are willing to walk alongside us on our journey no matter how long that journey takes.

Time as benchmarks. When your child dies, you will experience many firsts: the first dinner without them, the first school day without waving goodbye, the first year, the first time we go back to work, the first summer vacation with one less family member; the first birthday after the death, and so on. When we pass these benchmarks, we can breathe a sigh of relief. We have made it through. We are surviving, even though it is impossible to believe that we did it or even wanted to.

Time to reflect. We each need moments for ourselves, when we do not want to be with others or do activities we have always done, when we want to think about the loss that has changed our lives so irrevocably, when we want to reflect on "what now?" This does not mean we are running away; it simply means that to act as if nothing has happened does not work. When we realize we can accept what has happened, we are ready to re-enter the world we know. It will be a different world; we will have new priorities and goals; what was once important to us may no longer matter. That is okay. Change can be for the good also.

Time as a healer. The intensity we feel at the beginning of our loss will diminish with time and although the pain and hurt will never go away, we learn to deal with it, to live with the unanswered question, "Why me; why my child?" The grief will always be with you and sometimes, unexpectedly, for no good reason, your eyes will become watery and tears may fall as you remember. Do not be embarrassed. A wave of grief is a common occurrence. It will pass, and your life will continue with both special moments and private moments locked forever deep in your heart.

15. Choosing a Support Group vs. Reading Books

Why do some bereaved parents go to a grief support group?

- We need to be with people who understand what we are going through. Only someone who has been there can identify with us completely.
- We will find new friends and closer bonds than we ever thought possible.
- We can be ourselves there. We can cry when we need to and not worry about being embarrassed. We can hug others whether we know the person or not.
- We need to talk to someone who is a good listener as we remember our children and share the good memories.
- If we are further along, we feel a need to help others who are going through the same grief journey we are. Others were there for us when we needed them the most. Now we will be there for newer ones.
- We feel a need to do something positive out of a horrible tragedy. Helping others in their worst moment is one way.
- Because when we reach out to someone else, we also help ourselves.

Why do some parents read everything they can get their hands on?

- We turn to writings of others to find help and comfort. We may feel uncomfortable being around other bereaved parents and have a hard enough time dealing with our own problems and do not want to hear other's stories in a group setting.
- We read to see if others feel the same as we do. We want to read their stories and compare them to our own.
- We want confirmation that we are not crazy for how or what we feel.
- We want to learn techniques from experts to better our lives and help us on our grief journey.

We are so lost when this happens to us that sometimes we cannot even think straight. The experts who write about stages of grief and other topics allow us to understand better what we all go through.

Whether it is through a grief group, on your own, or through reading materials, each of us has our own way of moving forward with our lives after the worst possible thing that can happen to us becomes reality. Dealing with the loss of a child is a lifelong journey, and we should deal with it in whatever way is the most helpful to each one of us.

16. Writing About Your Grief

Three ways you can deal with grief through writings are

- **Journaling**
- **Affirmations**
- **Precious Conversations**

By **journaling** one can relate innermost thoughts as a release mechanism and go back to examine those feelings. Writing down raw feelings at this awful time and then looking back at it months or even years later can show how much growth has occurred.

I'm sorry I did not journal when my daughter died. However, I did a lot of writing; hence my first book. I can see now that if I had kept a journal, no matter how I was feeling at the time, I could have stepped aside and gotten a very different perspective of my situation.

Journaling allows us to write down spur of the moment thoughts and emotions in diary form. Sometimes I look back at my own book and think that if I had not written anything down, I would never have remembered all that took place during those dark days. I also look at the book and say to myself, "Gosh, did I write that? It's not bad at all!" I wonder if I could do as good and honest a job now that so much time has passed and the emotions are so different.

Journaling is a true measure of how one is feeling. One mother told me at a bereavement conference that journaling helped her understand the anger she felt towards the man who was driving drunk and smashed into her daughter's car, killing her instantly. The man walked away uninjured. "By focusing on my feelings, I could deal with what happened much better so that when I saw him in court, I was not a raving lunatic." Another mother hopes to put her journaling into book form so that other bereaved parents can glimpse her pain when her daughter died of a brain tumor and how she lived through those months while her child was still alive.

What can we say when journaling? We can talk about how we felt when our child died and how we lived through those first few months. Other suggestions are how we react to others now, what our child meant to us, a few good memories, what we think we might do for ourselves to move on, how we are coping, what drives us crazy, what others should know about us or our child, or any raving we have about what happened to our child. These are only suggestions. The most important thing is to write down what is in your heart. The words and emotions will just flow out. Put something down on paper every day.

In journaling, we are free to say what we want without any fear of recrimination. It is not necessary that anyone see your journal, but perhaps by showing it to others at the appropriate time, a deeper understanding between yourself and your spouse, your friends or your surviving children will occur.

If the idea of journaling with lots of writing seems overwhelming to you, begin each day with one or two lines that is a positive thought or **affirmation** for getting through the day. For example, *"Attitude is a little thing that can make a big difference,"* "I will not let my grief consume me," *or "I'm looking forward to a brighter tomorrow."* Make an effort to switch your thinking for the day from negative to positive using these or any other affirmations that may be helpful. By doing this continually, we can regain some control of our life and move past the pain that grief has brought to your life.

Another idea from a grief educator and facilitator in Arizona, Sandra Howlett, explores a process called "**precious conversations**" and here is what she says about it.

"One of the most painful parts of grief is the sense of absolute separation from loved ones," said Sandra, who has had over 15 years of personal experience and advanced training in dialogue journaling. "Parents often carry unwarranted guilt and regret causing them additional agony on top of their near unbearable sadness. Most people yearn for the opportunity to reach out to their children for at least one more conversation. Many grief-stricken parents visit psychics and mediums in an effort to connect with their children or other loved ones who have died. While this may be helpful, it is sometimes impractical, expensive and holds the potential for manipulation and fraud."

Precious Conversations is an experiential session that taps into the inner wisdom of the individual to facilitate a written dialogue between a participant and anyone they choose, living or dead. It is like having a conversation with a loved one.

Sandra incorporates dialogue journaling in bereavement support groups as well as one to one work with clients. It is a safe, simple process that opens hearts and offers comfort and reassurance. Participants are asked to suspend their skepticism and the first writing is stepping-stones, that is, key moments in your life. Once you have those moments, the next step is to explore dialoguing through journaling with the one to whom we want to communicate. Then you have a short guided meditation and finally write the dialogue conversation with the loved one. Participants can share if they want to or do not have to, but they do find there is still a connection there between them and the loved ones.

The following example shows how powerful and comforting dialogue journaling can be. One time Sandra met with a woman whose child died at 16 months. They met on the anniversary of the child's death. Sandra showed her this process and the parent felt very comforted and reassured when it was over. This parent was stuck in her grief and this process helped her say at the end, "I'm okay now."

Whatever your reason for journaling, writing affirmations or doing conversation writing, know that it can be good for you in your grief journey. I encourage you to begin today.

17. *Taking Care of Yourself*

When a child dies, the grief is intense. We become immobile and don't care about anything. We don't even want to think about anything except the child that we lost. Your number one priority now should be to take care of yourself. We may have other children or a spouse who need us or a job or activity may need your input.

Grief affects the mental, emotional, spiritual and physical parts of your body. This change in your life will drain you physically and exhaust you emotionally. Grief work is hard work, the hardest you will ever have to do. So how should we deal with these changes in our life while walking this difficult journey we call grief? Here are a few suggestions.

DEALING WITH CHANGES IN YOUR LIFE
- **Exercise**
- **Eat properly**
- **Get a good night's sleep**
- **Listen to music**
- **Read**
- **Volunteer**
- **Find a place of worship**
- **Reach out to friends or family**
- **Do a scrapbook or video of pictures**
-

Doing daily exercise is good for both your spirit and your body functions. A class in yoga or Pilates or both will help you physically and emotionally. It will release chemicals that are good for your body and give you that energy you so desperately need. If you don't have time to do a complete regimented program, try just walking for a minimum of 30 minutes a day at a 16-minute or better mile. Keeping fit will keep your body ready for the continued adjustment to loss.

Drink many fluids and force yourself to eat properly. A well-balanced diet with lots of water, fruits and vegetables will help your energy level and keep you healthy. Try some herbal tea for relaxation. Your body is under a tremendous amount of stress as you adjust to your loss.

A good night's sleep is important. Resting is good for any anxiety you may feel about your loss. Try not to take medication to sleep.

Listen to some meditation music or play some instrumental background music. You will be surprised at how music will help you to relax and gain a different perspective.

Read. Whether it is a comic book, a novel, a grief book or a magazine article, you will need to relax and relieve some tension during the day. If a specific grief book, you may come to understand your own reactions better as you go through your grief journey. Keep your mind active.

Volunteer in a hospital, church or school, or perhaps help a friend who is not well. When you do things for others, you will feel better about yourself and your own situation.

Find a place of worship and attend. This may be difficult for those who want to blame God for what happened to their child. You can restore your faith and help in your healing process by attending, sitting and listening.

Reach out to friends and family. We are not alone. There are many going through similar experiences. Find some of those people and share your thoughts and your child with them. If you are having trouble coping and think a grief therapist might be of help, seek one out. In doing so, make sure they understand and are helpful to your specific needs. A grief support group can help you through your journey and allows you to realize your feelings are normal.

If you feel you must do something related to your child, why not try a scrapbook or a video of pictures you have of them. It will be something you can always look at, now and in the future with fond memories.

You will survive this loss. It may take a year, two years, five years, but you will eventually work it out. Try some of these techniques and see if any of them are of help to you.

18. Coping List

The death of a child is the most unbearable loss of all. Everyone has his or her own timeline for grieving. Know that there is no set time limit to grieve, nor should one feel guilty about the time it takes. Everyone must do whatever is best for him or her. However, you will know when you are beginning to cope. Here are ten tips.

You know you are coping when:
- You can say your child's name without choking.
- Putting away your child's belongings does not mean putting him/her out of your life
- You accept your child has died but the love you shared will never die.
- The laughter you hear is your own.
- A smile plays on your lips when looking at photographs of your child.
- You are interested in matters outside of yourself.
- You remember to take care of yourself.
- You appreciate a beautiful sunrise or sunset, the small pleasures.
- Memories bring comfort and warmth instead of emptiness and pain.
- You realize you will always miss your child, but he/she is part of your life forever.

19. Rebuilding a Marriage After a Child Dies

Many couples who have experienced the death of their child may also experience a crisis in their marriage as a result. This untimely event can be an opportunity for growth bringing the two people closer together.

The belief that a bereaved couple is doomed to divorce is blown way out of proportion. In fact, a Compassionate Friends survey has indicated that only 4 percent of couples who divorce do so because of the child's death and that something else was wrong in the relationship before the child died. If the couple has always had a good marriage, typically that marriage will grow stronger, not collapse.

DEALING WITH CRISIS IN A MARRIAGE

- **Talk about the child**
- **Give each other space and time to grieve differently**
- **Talk to friends about your relationship**
- **Get a new perspective by going off on your own**
- **Please your spouse with activities he enjoys**
- **Review your day together**
- **Accept the death and learn to live together without your child**

Making your relationship a priority during this difficult time should be your goal. One way to do this is to talk about your child. Remember the good times, funny incidents. Laugh at something silly that your child did as well as remember any awards, honors and graduations that made you so proud. Don't dwell on how your child died. That is not going to bring him or her back. If you feel guilty about something, talk about it. If you are angry about something, talk about that also. Couples have a bond with their child that no one else can match and by talking about those bonds and your feelings, you may realize how very similar you feel or at least respect the opposite feelings of your partner.

The chance of both parents grieving the same is unlikely. Partners should allow each other the space to grieve at his/her own rate and in his/her own way. Personality, previous experiences, and your own style of grieving contribute to that respect of grieving space. If one partner wants to cry, that doesn't mean the other one has to cry. If one partner doesn't feel like going out, he or she shouldn't feel obligated to do so. If you can't decide what to make for breakfast, don't worry about it; your child died, you need time to adjust, and you eventually will.

A few other suggestions may work for you. Talk to friends about your relationship with your husband to ease the stress buildup. Perhaps they have a good resource for any problems. You may also need to express feelings about your loss to friends that you are not ready to discuss with your spouse.

Sometimes when one partner feels bad, going off on your own for a few hours or a day may give you a new perspective. Do not bring your spouse down or make them suffer with sarcastic comments or harmful accusations just because you feel miserable.

Look for ways you can please your spouse to ease some of his/her pain. Do some activity with him/her that you do not usually do but know the other would like you to do. Make a special meal that the other enjoys eating. Alternatively, do something related to your child that up until now you have not been able to do.

At the end of the day, coming together is important. Review with your spouse what has happened that day, how you are feeling and what you are thinking. You will more than likely learn a lot about your partner during this period of your life more than at any other time.

Time is also a great healer. As time passes you will discover a sense of acceptance of what has happened to you and your spouse and, hopefully. have the willingness to learn to find new ways of living your life 'together' without your child.

20. Forgiveness As It Relates to Grief

Are you able to forgive someone who has wronged you? If you were the parent of a student in the Columbine massacre, if you lost loved ones on 9/11, or if your child was one of two students killed by a drunk driver in a horrific car accident, how forgiving would you be towards the person who was responsible?

When we suffer the death of someone we love, we experience mental, emotional and physical distress. Because of this, we might feel anger or resentment.

In the case of the drunk driver, one mother has forgiven the driver; one father cannot.

From the mother: "I can't live my life with hate and anger in my heart; I just can't." From the father: "If I forgive him, then my son died for nothing." Both of these parents now work on committees against drunk driving and give talks to groups and students.

The mother has gone one-step further. She and the drunk driver who killed her son speak together. They speak across the entire country. The driver shares the fact that every day he realizes what he is responsible for having done. The two embrace onstage and sometimes shock and anger other parents in the audience. Again, some agree with what the mother is doing; others do not. The mother says she can't deal with this without forgiving him.

The driver comes up for parole in a couple of years. Both the mother and father whose children died in this accident disagree as to whether he should go free. The mother wants the boy to have a life, a family; the father is angry that the driver will probably get to, but his son won't get any of that.

"It's just not in my heart to forgive," says the father. He can't do it. They have come to opposite conclusions.

An impaired driver killed my daughter. Because he wasn't found, part of my closure has always eluded me. I believe I am personally better off this way. There is no forgiveness and no revenge in me to deal with since I do not know who this man is or what the actual circumstances were before the accident.

Avoiding forgiveness can be detrimental to our healing. However, forgiveness will not make us feel better immediately. Studies show that people who forgive are happier and healthier than those who hold resentments. Therefore, we can benefit greatly from forgiving others. We may never forget what happened to our child, but we can still forgive. In the long term what forgiveness can do is restore valuable relationships and that has a long term, satisfying quality to it."

Forgiveness is born in part from the experience of someone else's pain. We want to understand the other person. We need to let go of our anger at this person. When someone harms us, we get upset emotionally and physically, but by forgiving, our health is better.

Look inside yourself and try to understand how you would react if it was you in any of these circumstances and see if forgiveness, the healthier way, is the path you would choose. Remember, forgiveness doesn't happen immediately. It is a journey of the heart.

21. The Acronym TEAR in a Grief Journey

Grief work can be summarized by the acronym TEAR:

T = To accept the reality of your loss
E = Experience the pain of your loss
A = Adjust to the environment without the deceased
R = Reinvest in the new reality

This makes a lot of sense to me. All four of these are important if you are to move through your grief journey.

I remember at first when my daughter died, it was like she had just gone away for a while and that I would see her again. I was denying the loss, probably because I couldn't believe this had happened to me. It took three years before I realized she wouldn't be coming back. That is probably the reason that when people ask me which year was the worst, I always respond: the third year.

Losing a child is like no other loss we will ever experience. The feelings that go along with this are horrific and almost unbearable. I brought this child into the world. I nourished and watched her grow. She was my future and now both our futures are gone. These are the thoughts that might run through one's mind, along with many others, most prominent being, "Why did this happen? What did I do to deserve this? Why me?"

During this time, we don't feel like doing anything. Time has stopped for now. As time passes, we learn to deal with the death and live one-minute, one-hour and one-day at a time. It is almost as if we must relearn to get out of bed, get dressed, eat and go to work. I always think of the woman who had to learn how to function again after the death of her son. She sat at home day after day staring at his picture. She didn't get dressed or go to work, she didn't cook for her husband and she didn't even acknowledge her husband when he came home from work. She lost her job and almost lost her husband too. Finally, her husband forced her to listen to him. He explained that he was suffering also, but he could no longer hold up both of them. He said he was going to leave if she didn't try to help herself. She realized he was serious and knew that would be the final blow. They began grief therapy. It took them a long time to work it all out, but with the help of family and wonderful friends, they both became survivors and are still together, working at having as normal a life as possible.

Life does indeed go on, and it goes on without your child. We did many things with our child that we may no longer want to attempt to do. When a friend invites us to a baseball game, your first thought may be, "I did that with my son. I can't ever go to another baseball game." We will find that if we do go, it will definitely be difficult, but when it's over, we can look back and breathe a sigh of relief that we made it through. It is these "firsts" that are the most difficult, and there will be many firsts in your new life.

A niece was graduating a few months after Marcy died. Her parents invited me to attend the ceremonies. I knew I could not go. I knew I would break down and cry and did not want to in front of others. I asked to excuse me; I just could not attend. The family understood. Now, many years later I do go to other events and celebrations. Sure, I think of Marcy and may shed a few tears, but I also have happy thoughts of how proud I was of her. Enough time has passed, and I have adjusted to an environment without my daughter. It takes a lot of time and effort to live in a world without your child.

I had to define new goals and new priorities in my life after the death of my child. I am now a different person and the new me needs to share with others who have had the same experience as I have, to help others who need a friendly ear, and to share with others newfound wisdom about life and death. Throwing yourself into your daily routine, exercising, and eating right all help to make us feel better. Call friends and family; they all care about our well-being.

Dealing with death and the aftermath is very stressful. Rest and do not overtax yourself. Do not be upset if you start crying at any moment. It is a normal part of the grieving process and will happen often. It will also release all the tension of the day or week that has built up. Don't feel guilty about it.

Lastly, don't forget to do something for yourself. It could be shopping, walking, or just reading a good book. The grief journey is hard work and we need to do whatever helps us cope best.

22. *How Men Grieve*

Fathers grieve differently with different emotions in the loss of a child. I believe this to be true. Here is some information I gathered on how men grieve after losing a child.

According to research, bereaved fathers put their grief into a compartment separate from the rest of their lives. Because they feel they need to protect their families, they submerge their own grief. They dislike intense emotion and feel that talking about the emotion only makes it worse. They deal with grief by thinking about something else, by doing something else and when they do cry, they cry alone.

Men do not want to talk about a death. They do not want to talk at bereavement meetings and do not even like to come to them. If they do come, they say they are doing it just to please their wives and make them happy. Men feel grief as deeply as women do. It is just that men, because of the image that a man should be strong and somewhat macho, grow up with the idea of big boys do not cry. Deep down men want to talk to other men about their grief, but find they must do it in a safe environment.

Men submerge their own grief to take care of their families. You are the father; you have all the answers, others say. Fathers wonder what they can say to make everything better so their families do not suffer. How can they fix it? After a death, there are many things to do, so one must be strong. Crying shows weakness, they say.

Fathers deal with grief by distracting themselves with jobs, hobbies, duties, pleasures. Some even go back to work after a week so they do not have to sit around in the depths of their grief. They plunge themselves into work to just keep going.

In the end, fathers will tell you they become more sensitive to other people's feelings, more aware of pain in others. The one thing a father may miss if they have an only child is a sense of lineage, of their children carrying their names into the future.

Here are a few suggestions that can provide a respite from the stress:

- Do your favorite activity and daily exercise as part of taking time for yourself.
- Avoid new responsibilities. You have enough on your mind now
- It is healthy to cry, so don't be embarrassed when you do.
- Talk with your spouse and other bereaved fathers about the feelings you have at this time. **Let the important people in your life know you are hurting and let them help you.**
- Don't expect to feel better immediately. Take your time.
- Seek professional help if needed.
- Give yourself permission to grieve and realize everyone grieves differently
- Cherish the happy memories of your child. Don't focus on anything negative.
- Read all you can about grief, particularly a book by a bereaved father. Five suggestions are *When Life Goes on* by Jimmy Egan; *Andy's Mountain* by Dwight Patton; *Letters To My Son* by Mitch Carmody; *Heartworks* by Jerre Petersen; and *Into the Valley and Out Again* by Richard Edler.

23. Inappropriate Responses To Bereaved Parents

When on your grief journey, you may hear people say things to you that are not appropriate at all. Perhaps that person was only trying to comfort you or has never lost a child and has no idea what you are feeling or going through. Certain phrases and sentences to others may seem like a way to show they care and are thinking about you, but all it really does is make you mad. Some of those phrases and my reactions (in italic type) include:

"Your child is in a better place." *No, she is not. She should be right here with me.*

"Aren't you over it yet?" *I will never get over this. In time, I may be able to learn to live with the loss, but I'll never get over it completely, nor will I ever forget.*

"I know how you feel. My dog died last year." *Please do not compare your dog to my child. You may have loved your dog very much, but a dog is not a human being, born and nurtured from your body.*

"You can have more children." *Maybe I can, maybe I cannot; maybe I cannot bear the thought of ever going through this again, but having another child would not be to replace the one I lost.*

"God never gives you more than you can bear." *Why did God do this to me at all? Am I being punished for some reason?*

"Time will heal your hurt." *Time may ease the pain somewhat, but heal me completely? Never! I will always ache for my child and what we have both lost.*

"I understand." *No, you do not, unless you have also lost a child. Nothing compares. A child should never die before a parent.*

"At least she isn't suffering." *She is suffering. I am suffering. She had so much more living to do, things to accomplish. No matter what would have happened to her physically, she would have dealt with it and continued living a full life.*

"Crying won't bring her back." *Crying is a healthy emotion to cleanse your body physically and mentally. No, I will not get her back, but holding back emotions cause more damage. If I want to scream and rant, that is okay also.*

"It's time to get rid of her clothes and belongings." *When I feel the time is right, I will take some action. It could be a month, a year or even 5 years. I will do it in my own time. I will never get rid of everything. I could never part with some items.*

Be patient with these people and do not let these common phrases get to you. DO try to let others know what you personally think is not appropriate to say to a bereaved parent, whether it is you or someone else.

24. What To Do with Your Child's Possessions

When your child dies, you must eventually make decisions about what to do with your child's possessions. Certain items you will always keep...that cute drawing a 3-year-old made of what he/she perceives as his house...that first hand print...that certificate the child gave you saying you are 'the greatest mother/father in the world.' You will treasure those items forever. Other items you have to make decisions about are the clothing, the jewelry, the trophies and awards.

Should you keep everything? Should you give everything away? Some parents gain much comfort during the grief process from seeing, touching and wearing their child's items. Others find it too painful. Do what feels right for you WHEN you wish to do it. Do not let family or friends tell you what or when to do it. It is important not to

---

Should you keep everything? Should you give everything away? What is the right thing to do when dealing with your child's possessions?

---

dispose of items too quickly as later you may regret it. There is nothing wrong with keeping whatever you want to keep forever!

I kept most of my daughter's jewelry because I like to wear it. It makes me feel so close to her and she had such wonderful taste in jewelry. A few earrings I wanted some of her friends to have, and I asked them to choose what they wanted. I did the same with her clothes, keeping some, giving some to her friends who were her same size, and giving the rest to Goodwill. Wearing the clothing is also comforting, although her perfume smell has long since disappeared. A leather jacket she bought in Italy and a sweater jacket I wear in chilly weather to this day still bring compliments for their designs. As I wear them out a little, I can only hope that they will continue to last for quite a while to come.

I have only one blouse left and thought I would turn it into a

Carrie Bear. Carrie Pike at www. carriebears@juno.com takes clothing and will make bears out of it and even put pictures on the front of the bears. I packaged up the last blouse and was just about to mail it. Then a strange thing happened. I could not let it out of my hands. "The last blouse," I kept saying. "I can't. I can't." In the end, I couldn't mail the blouse, took it out and hung it back up. Maybe one day I will be ready, but then again, maybe not. Surviving grief certainly has its difficulties.

There is no correct timing for doing something with your child's belongings. You will know when you are ready for a change. One important thing to remember is to store items you want to keep in a place with a good temperature, so they aren't ruined. If there is anything you want to display, trophy cases, display cases or a memory box are helpful. Alternatively, you may just want to keep it in your closet to take out from time to time as you remember special moments and events.

The most important thing to remember is that putting your loved ones things away does not mean putting them out of your life. Your child will always remain a part of you.

25. Additional Ways To Help the Bereaved

Many ideas can help bereaved parents cope. You may have a friend who is just starting out on his or her grief journey, and it is hard enough for them just to get out of bed in the morning. They need comfort; they need you to see that they make it through the day. You have been there. You understand what they are feeling. Here are some of the things you can do for them.

- Send a sympathy card or note to the parents, saying how sorry you are and including a happy anecdote you remember about the child. Remembering good times is what you want to emphasize with these parents.
- If in the same town as the parents, go over to their home and give the parents big hugs. Say nothing or just say, "I'm sorry." There is nothing more soothing or meaningful to a bereaved parent when they do not have to explain anything and know you understand what they are going through.
- Cry with the bereaved parent. Parents may have trouble letting go, so you can show them others feel as they do and want to relieve a buildup of emotions.
- Offer to help them with daily tasks when visiting. They may need you to shop for them, go to the cleaners, or pick up their other children from school.
- Let the parents talk if they want to. Most parents don't want their child to be forgotten and talking about them

relieves that fear. Acknowledge the child yourself by remembering an event or moment you were involved in with the child or you have heard the parents speak of previously.

- Attend the child's memorial service or encourage the parents to have one for the child. A service will allow friends and family to speak of the child and relive good times.

- Respect a parent's grieving time. Some bereaved parents need a few months, a year or even longer to reconnect with the world. Give them that time, but be there for them no matter how long it takes.

- Accept that the parents are different. Tragedy changes us. We have new priorities and goals. The price of oil may no longer be of any importance nor is the fact that city taxes may go up next year.

- Make sure the parents take care of themselves physically. See that they get exercise. Have them join you on a walk; invite them out to eat a good meal; encourage them to try to get enough sleep and stay healthy.

- Try to remember the child's birthday with a call or card. The parents will never forget, and it will show them their child was important to others also.

- Encourage the parents to seek a support group to help them get through this if you think they would be receptive to such an idea.

- When you feel enough time has passed, try to get the parents to start a scholarship in the child's name, plant a tree at his/her school or give to charity in his/her name. Building memorials for the child will help others remember them also.

26. Moving To the Other Side of Grief

A friend of mine told me recently that she is moving on with her life after her only son died in 2006. Her voice sounded upbeat. Her spirits were soaring. Only good things are happening now, and she is enjoying watching her grandchildren growing up, graduating and marrying. She also has a good relationship with her daughter-in-law who just remarried. "Now," she says, "I want to figure out what I want to do with the rest of my life."

When this first happened, I could not convince her she would survive the loss. She told me that she realizes now what she misses the most besides her son's presence in her life. "I miss the conversations we had, the fighting back and forth, most times with a good ending. I miss the exchange of loving phrases. I miss the laughter."

I tried to make a coffee date to see her and was finally successful. Her calendar was busy with whatever activities she enjoys and people she enjoys being with. She will find her way, I am confident, and I am happy she has come so far.

Sadly, her husband is not in the same place. He cannot get past his son's death or the way he died. He is uncomfortable going to a grief group; he did see a counselor for a year. I'm sure he feels a lot of anger and rage at what happened and probably asks himself (as most of us do) "Why me?" I hope that he too, can do it on his own, but he is an example of why I write these articles, hoping that something will click for him too. One day I'm sure it will. It will just take him longer. No two people grieve alike or for the same amount of time. I'm convinced he will come out on the other side of grief as my friend has.

This couple is a good example of how men and women, husbands and wives, are not necessarily in the same place after the death of their child. They should not concentrate on how the child died or that they could not save them. If they can talk about the child remembering the good times and the loving relationship with the child, their communication can help each other accept their loss, cope with their life as it is now and eventually get to the other side of grief.

27. Confronting Negative Statements

At a recent dinner, I sat next to a woman who knew Marcy through others. We were never very friendly, although I have known her for many years. She turned to me and said, "You know, it is very sad that Marcy died, but you should have had more children. Then it would not have been so tragic for you. You would have at least had other children in your life."

I was stunned that anyone would say that to a bereaved mother, no matter how long ago the child had died. Was she trying to comfort me? Did she think she was showing me she cared about me? I felt insulted. I wanted to say, "You stupid person. You have obviously never had a child die nor know anything about it."

I kept my voice calm and said, "Another child doesn't replace the one you lost, nor does another child even ease the pain of the loss. Each child is a separate individual, loved unconditionally." Besides, I thought to myself, I could never bear the thought of ever going through this again with another child, although there are many parents who have lost more than one child and survived.

I explained to this woman that I did try to have more than one child. I lost one in a miscarriage and told not to get pregnant again due to health reasons. "Oh," was all she could say.

As I looked at the woman who just turned to talk to someone else, I could see she never for one minute thought she had said anything offensive. Thinking about it, she probably voiced what others only think but never say.

"We assume you are all better now; it's been a year, so why don't you try to have more children?"

When I told this story at a bereavement meeting recently, most rolled their eyes, shook their heads, and looked disgusted. Then a few began telling me their own stories, some very similar to mine. One bereaved mother after a year of grieving went out to lunch with some friends. She related that one of her friends said, "We assume you are all better now; it's been a year, so why don't you try to have more children? At least then our children will be close in age and grow up together." Angered, the mother told this so-called friend that she did not manufacture children at a moment's notice; she was not over the loss; and it was really none of her business.

Still another mother at the meeting related how, at a wedding, an old friend said, "Why so sad looking?" She said she had just been thinking of her son and how much she knew he would like to be there. The response was "Oh, get over it. It's been long enough; it's time to move on." The bereaved mother said simply and calmly, "I am trying to move on, but it's difficult at times." She then turned around and left the party. "I cried all the way home," said the mother.

"Sometimes people just don't know what to say and so they try to say something they think will be comforting and unfortunately, often times, it is not comforting at all but very hurtful," said a bereaved parent. "It takes experiencing one's own loss to possibly begin to understand this."

"It's horrifying how stupid and selfish some people are..." said one mother, when asked if she is having more children.

"There are other times, she continued, that people just really aren't sensitive at all. Like the wedding example, she was having fun and had no presence of mind to realize that someone who lost a child might still be grieving at an occasion like that. I think people forget that when we have lost a child, it is always present in our minds and some of the simplest daily experiences bring sad reminders that they are gone. For some, they do not want to dredge up your grief feelings so they try to avoid it by being all bubbly and happy around you…as if that will help. Let's face it…they know that at a moment's notice it could be them and they don't want to face that!"

Finally, another mother thinks it is horrifying how unbelievably stupid and selfish some people are. "I've been asked more than once if we are having more children. Even my husband contemplated it in a moment of irrational grief, but at least he had the excuse of desperately needing his little boy back. I just cannot fathom how people regurgitate at others without actually examining what they are saying beforehand. I've decided that next time anyone probes my reproductive life I'll just say, 'My tubes are tied,' and leave it at that."

The grief journey is hard enough without others attempting to tell us how to live our lives. They have no idea what it is like to lose a child and I, personally, hope they never have to be in that situation.

A formal set of rules to educate people as to how to be compassionate, how to react, what to say, and particularly what not to say to a bereaved parent would make our journey a little less stressful.

28. Grief in the Workplace

Returning to work after the death of a child can be difficult for both the employee and the employer. A total estimation of $37.5 billion in lost productivity is attributed to the death of a loved one. No matter where the grieving individual is located on the organizational chart, any business will suffer from the loss of productive work time, mistakes on the job, and the disillusionment of other employees who witness the struggle. Staff turnover means costly recruitment and training. The grief following the death of a child is intense, long-lasting and complex. This poses unique challenges for the one grieving and for the employer.

The Grieving Parent
- May have difficulty making work decisions
- Relay funeral arrangements to the office
- Ask for some time off from your job
- Request a grief counselor if necessary
- Mention child's name so employees will feel comfortable talking about him/her

Besides the obvious that work is the last thing on your mind during this time, you are probably dreading facing your co-workers. You may have difficulty making work decisions, be frustrated, depressed, irritable, and disinterested in work related details. You are probably worried about starting to cry in front of the work force. The sensitivity of people within the work environment has a profound effect on the recovery process.

Take some steps to ease the transition back to work. Call the office and tell them what has happened. Relay funeral arrangements to those close to you who may want to attend. Do not feel you must tell every detail about the circumstances of the death.

Ask for some time off from your job, or ask to return to work for only partial days at the beginning of your grief journey. You may also need help with certain projects at work; do not forget to show your appreciation for that help. Make sure you know the policies on bereavement leave and ask for whatever time you think you need.

You may also want to request a grief counselor to meet with the other employees and answer any questions they may have about how they can help or what to expect. That specialist can also teach other employees a little about the grief process so they are familiar with what to do when you are having a bad day.

More than anything, bereaved parents want to talk about their child, whether it is at home, at a meeting or in their workplace. You may want to talk about your child at work, but do not overdo it. Other employees need to be aware that you probably need to talk in order to heal. Mention the child's name so others will know it is okay for them to talk about the child also.

Above all else, keep the lines of communication open so your employer will know how to deal with the situation also.

What the employer can do

- Work with employee to adjust time schedule
- Show compassion
- Relate funeral arrangements
- Mention support groups that may help
- Make workplace part of the healing process

Many responsible employers are asking what they can do. Employers should relate funeral arrangements to everyone and even try to attend if possible to show support. It is also important to know the different cultural customs that some employees may practice.

They need to be interested and listen to their employee so that communication is not a problem. Work with the employee, give more time if needed to complete a task or adjust work hours for the bereaved parent. Be aware there is no precise timetable for recovery. By showing support and caring, the employer is making the bereaved parent feel more at ease when it is time to come back to the workplace. Showing compassion is the key here.

The best response when an employee comes back to work is just to say, "I'm so sorry." Bereaved parents do not want to hear any platitudes such as "God only takes the good ones" or "You can have more children."

Do not be afraid to mention support groups that may help the bereaved. There are many out there and it depends on the way the child died as to which one they might want to attend. Do not assume the bereaved parent knows all about them. Check them out yourself by going to the Compassionate Friends site or Hospice site. They would be more than happy to direct you to the right source.

If you are a bereaved parent and you believe your workplace could use some assistance, do not be afraid to offer your own advice or see to it that someone else offers it. There are organizations and professionals out there that can create an environment where the workplace is part of the healing grief process.

29. A Brief Meeting with Another Bereaved Parent

A friend called a few weeks ago, said a friend of hers had lost a son suddenly, and felt her friend needed to talk to someone who had gone through similar circumstances. My friend was worried about her friend. I told her I would be happy to talk to her friend, which I did, and we set up a date to have breakfast and meet.

I do so enjoy meeting other bereaved parents, and I'm sure you would too. We hugged; we knew what each other was feeling, no matter if one year or 15 years. I looked at her face. She wore no makeup, and I realized it was because she did not really care what others thought of her. She is her own person: independent, knows who she is and in control of her feelings. As we spoke, I also saw how eye makeup would not have worked well on her. Tears formed a lot, although never overflowing.

This was not her first tragedy. Her husband died in a plane crash over 35 years ago at age 36, and she has never remarried. I did not question whether she had anyone special in her life now. I did learn that she travels quite a bit and is a history and geography buff, so that when I would mention a place, she could pinpoint it exactly on a map and discuss the area, whether she had been there or not. She has one daughter, who she is close to, and some grandchildren. She is lucky in that respect.

Her son fell sick one day, went to the doctor and finally the hospital. "They missed the diagnosis," she told me. "They should have done a blood test while in the hospital." Then they would have known her son contracted a rare and fatal virus. The pain started in his neck, and he was dead in less than 24 hours. If they had done the blood test, they probably could have saved him. It was a sudden death, just like my daughter, although in a completely different way, but sudden nevertheless. Sudden death is hard to accept. You never dream it could happen to a loved one.

She talked about meeting Elizabeth Kubler Ross and the books on grief that she wrote. We compared notes and agreed on most aspects. She talked about not wanting to go to a grief group, like myself. She discussed people she believes hide in their religion. She has never once asked, "Why me? What good does it do," she told me. I agreed.

She seems to be on the right path. She will continue to have good and bad days as we all do and will, all the days of our lives. Her son will always be in her thoughts as my daughter will always be in mine. Our feelings and thoughts are more similar than I thought they might be at first. It both surprises and pleases me.

It is heart wrenching for me to hear another bereaved parent's story. They are all so sad, and I empathize with the parents. I understand every feeling they are going through because I have been there also. I learn from every parent I meet and grow from the experience. I often say that I have a purpose here on earth and that is to do what I can for any parent who needs to talk, who needs to cry and who needs a hand to hold. If given the opportunity to meet another bereaved parent, take it and make the most of it. Confirming through another bereaved parent that his or her thoughts, reactions and feelings are similar to yours can be very comforting.

We talked for hours, and probably could have continued, except that I had to leave for another appointment. We hugged again, this time with a little more feeling of, "I'm so sorry this has happened to both of us." We planned to meet again, soon. After all, we have one thing in common that will always bind us together...our children, who are no longer with us.

30. Signs from Our Children Help Us Cope

Mothers have an uncanny way of knowing exactly about their child's health, and in Susan's case, it was gratifying to have the head of pediatrics realize it when he said to her "You knew all the time, didn't you?" Susan did. He had no clue how she could have known that her daughter was dying because the doctors kept reiterating until the day the baby died that she would be fine.

Susan's baby was born with multiple physical birth defects and was in and out of the hospital many times during the first 8 months of her life before she died. Doctors insisted that when she got a little older they could operate on her and she'd be fine. Little was known in those days about many of her defects and doctors assumed wrongly that she would be okay.

Susan spent as much time as possible with the baby. Things just got worse and Susan knew. She went to a spiritual counselor to talk about a feeling she had that her baby wouldn't make it. The counselor went into a trance, told her the baby would not live long and described the physical disabilities, hitting everything correctly. Susan believes this counselor felt everything the baby felt as she was dying. What the counselor said validated Susan's feelings and helped her cope.

Susan says that her baby was her greatest teacher. She believes the baby was an old soul—all knowing. She explained that it was as if the baby was looking into her soul. A peace surrounded the baby that Susan had never felt before.

The spiritual counselor said the baby wanted to learn one more thing before she died: how to accept love without being able to give it. She couldn't physically put her arms out to be held and she couldn't give anything back. She had a huge presence about her that Susan will never forget.

Susan remembers one incident in the hospital right before the baby died that confirmed her belief that people, on some level, know they're leaving, even little ones. The baby put her arms up, crying as if she wanted to be held, something she had never been able to do before. A nurse Susan had never seen before, sitting in the corner of the room, said to her, "Do you want to hold the baby?" She had never been able to hold her before because of all the complications and disabilities. She picked her up and could see in her baby's eyes that she was trying to tell her something. Then the baby started gasping, and she had to put her down. The baby died later that night.

To this day, Susan believes the nurse in the room was an angel, and the baby was telling her goodbye and that everything was okay. She believes it was an amazing experience, one she will never forget. Many have had unexplained experiences where children have sent parents signs with whispers of love.

The death of the baby ended her marriage, but Susan admits that she was in the marriage for all the wrong reasons. Susan found help with the Center for Living with Dying, Hospice and learning Reiki, an ancient Japanese hands-on healing modality meaning soul power and reminding us of our ability to heal ourselves.

Susan continues to work in the grief field helping others. She has come to understand the meaning of her life and her purpose here on earth. She believes it was because of a small baby who came into her life for a very short but meaningful time, a child who taught Susan about unconditional love.

Other parents have spoken about butterflies landing on their shoulders and sensing it is their child telling them they are always there with the parent and not to worry about them.

Still another parent told me of waking up in the middle of the night, hearing their child's voice and seeing an image at the end of the bed for a brief second.

"I sometimes smell my daughter's perfume in the room, as though she has been there watching over me at night," said one mother.

I have heard a father speak about his son, who died from a brain tumor, and the messages of love and remembrances sent to him in different ways. This father believes his son is part of all the unexplainable incidents that have surrounded his life since the son's death. One in particular dealt with his son, very sick at the time, doing a very strange drawing. The father looked at it, didn't really know what it was, but put it with other ones he had done. Some time later, his other son did the same drawing, never having seen the first one and not even understanding why he did the drawing. To the father, it was a message from his son, no longer here, willing the brother to do the drawing.

Personally, I have not experienced these, but do not discount those who have. What I have discovered is I sometimes talk like my daughter and saying things in the same way she did in the past, and I catch my breath at how similar we sound.

Experiences such as these are fairly common among those who have lost a child or any loved one. They can also be very spiritually and emotionally healing. Are these just coincidences or real? That is not something we can say for sure. What we do know is that although we cannot always explain these happenings, they offer reassurance and comfort to parents.

We know and believe that wherever we are, our children are always with us, in our minds and in our hearts. Although not all of us have had these experiences, our children's spirits live on within us forever.

(Portions of Susan's story were condensed from one of the 25 stories in my book first grief book *I Have No Intention of Saying Good-bye.*)

31. Why Did My Child Choose Suicide?

Why? That is the eternal question for a parent whose child completes suicide. Why did they do this to themselves and their families?

According to psychologist, speaker and therapist Maurice Turmel, PhD, in an Ezine article he wrote on *Suicide Grief,* death due to suicide is probably the most complex grieving experience we ever have to deal with. A death by suicide can be because

- A person is mad at someone else and has chosen to punish him or her for some misbehavior
- A person is feeling desperate, and they have amplified those feelings with alcohol or drugs, leading to depression and the willingness to act
- A person feels their inner pain is unbearable and no one can help them, and they refuse to be helped

Statistics and surveys show that parents of suicide victims suffer a more intense grief for a much longer period than most other causes of child deaths. Suicide is the third leading cause of death for 15-24 year olds behind accidents and homicides. It is disturbing also to note that it is the fourth leading cause of death for children 10-14.

For other members of your family, the following can be warning signs of suicide, and knowing them may prevent another tragedy. Keep in mind that some of these are also similar to normal adolescent behavior and could just possibly look like destructive behavior but is not.

- Poems, essays and drawings referring to death
- Talking about death or suicide
- Overwhelming sense of guilt, shame or reflection
- Withdrawal from interacting with friends and family
- Plans ways to kill himself/herself
- Begins to take risks
- Changes in eating or sleeping patterns
- Has attempted suicide in the past
- Severe drop in school grades
- Expresses worries that nobody cares about him or her
- Dramatic changes in personality and behavior
- Begins to give away possessions
- Spends time online interacting with people who glamorize suicide
- Shows signs of depression
- Shows signs of substance abuse

Other factors that may contribute to the large number of teen suicides includes: divorce of parents, violence in the home, inability to find success at school, feelings of worthlessness, rejection by friends, death of someone close to them and suicide of a friend.

Parents of a child who has completed suicide are consumed with overwhelming grief, anger at the child for doing this, shock at the finality of it, confusion as to why this has happened and guilt over the fact that they could have caused this outcome. What could they have done to save this child? Was it their fault? Did they say or do something that pushed them over the edge? Why would someone we love do that to themselves and what was going on in their mind that this was the only way out?

The questions run through one's mind for a very long time. To think this was somehow your fault is absurd. We never had that power over them and that character flaws, genetic dispositions and numerous other reasons lead a person to suicide, none of which have anything to do with you as a parent.

Know that there is very little chance that you could have saved your child unless you were actually there to stop them or they have come to you as a last hope. Those determined to do this act will eventually succeed and all the talk, pleading, and begging will do little good.

It is unlikely that your child committed suicide to hurt you or to get even. He or she likely did it because there was no escape for the anguish and torment he/she felt, and it was the only way to escape the pain. It seems impossible to us that the child was so miserable or felt so unloved and hopeless that suicide was the only option. It is important to realize that you may never know the reasons for what has happened and you will have to accept and live with that.

One mother after a long period of therapy, what if's and screaming at her dead child about why she had chosen to end her life, realized that her daughter alone had made her choice, whether right or wrong, and it was not for her, as a mother, to judge that choice.

Janice Harris Lord in her book *No Time for Goodbyes* says that suicide is little understood by the public. Some people think that only severely mentally or emotionally ill people kill themselves and that the tendency is inherited. Others think suicide is purely environmental, that you or someone else drove your loved one to it. Either of these erroneous conclusions can cause people to shun the family. To avoid these stigmas, some choose to live a lie about the suicide, but that can complicate grieving, believing one thing on the inside and telling a story on the outside. Those who live lies tend to get sick. They can get depressed. They do not want to talk about the truth.

"The best prescription for recovery," according to Dr. Turmel, "is talking realistically and sharing your feelings with good friends, family, professional counselors or clergymen." "A good book or audio resource to help you deal with your feelings and emotions will also help. Joining a suicide support group will help you deal with your feelings, anger and guilt."

You will never have a satisfactory answer to "Why?" However, you can heal your own grief. "Don't try and tough this one out; you'll only become more depressed as a result," he said. "Don't repeat the mistake that drove your child to suicide. Give yourself every opportunity to heal and gain acceptance over an event you had no control of."

32. Accepting Others' Beliefs During Grief

"How could God have done this to me?"

"My God is a cruel God or he never would have let this happen?"

"It is my faith that has gotten me through this ordeal."

"I don't ever want to hear again, 'God only takes the good ones.'"

When the death of a child occurs in the family, many experience a faith in God they have never known before. They cling to the belief that they will reunite one day with their loved one. They may also say that because they believe in God, He will ease their suffering. Others look upon God as letting them down by allowing their loved one to die. Still others are confused about God's place in all this.

We hear the word "God" at a funeral service when a death occurs, in sympathy cards, from friends, relatives and even strangers.

We will find people saying things like, "God made sure that your child did not suffer." On a personal level I ask, why did my child have to suffer at all; why did this have to happen? I heard this comment from a very compassionate woman friend, who I know meant no harm and only wanted to ease my mind after the car accident that killed my daughter. My friend continued, "Would you have wanted your child to have been incapacitated all her life with you taking care of her? She's better off being with God." I thought to myself, what in the world makes her think she would have been in bad shape. A second thought quickly surfaced. I would have wanted her to be alive in any condition, and yes, I would have taken care of her.

I would have preferred my friend simply express her condolences to me, but I knew she was a religious person and her faith sustained her in everything she did. When she found out she had cancer, she was accepting of the fact she did not have long to live and used her remaining time to do what she referred to as God's work.

Others may say to bereaved parents, "You don't have to grieve too long; you'll be with your daughter eventually." That does not mean that I have to agree with a statement like this. I have a choice. I can get mad, or I can decide this is just an easy answer to something not understandable to many. I have chosen the latter.

An irritating phrase that bereaved parents do not want to hear is "God would want you to forgive," which someone might say if your loved one is murdered and the offender goes on trial. If you believe that the Higher Being of your faith can handle your anger and rage and take the tears away as they talk about heaven or eternal life, you are entitled to do so. If you do not believe any of that, try to explain your feelings. Everyone is entitled to his or her own beliefs.

In the book *No Time for Goodbyes* author Janice Harris Lord says, "The role of a Higher Being in what happened to you is your own faith decision. If you believe this was meant to be, that's fine. If it doesn't make sense, try to understand that those who say what they do, mean well and are sharing their own faith decision and not trying to hurt you."

On the other side of the fence, those who were once religious may lose all faith, blaming God for letting this death occur and swear they will never go into a church again. That is an emotional decision and could change with time. Others say that after-death spiritual experiences where their loved ones have communicated with them are emotionally and spiritually healing to them. Finally, others believe that their faith in God sustains them as they endure their suffering.

Some good guidelines to follow during this fragile time in your life:

- Don't discuss God with religious people who use this as an answer to complex questions. Their faith journey may have been different from yours.

- Find someone who has had an experience similar to yours who also has a meaningful religious faith and ask how their faith is helpful to them, whether you end up agreeing or not.
- Contact a religious counselor who has special training in accepting and dealing with grief.

Be accepting of others and their beliefs, even in your darkest hour, shows progress in your grief journey.

33. Message of Hope

One mother, Francine, who I know quite well, lost her only child, Valerie, more than 20 years ago. In a recent writing for a bereavement newsletter, she offers hope to those who are just beginning their grief journey. I find that it can be very comforting to those newly bereaved and even those a few years down the road to hear from others on how they have survived and moved forward with their lives doing new and useful projects. (That is how my first book came about.) I am pleased, as is Francine, to include her honest appraisal of how she felt, what she did with her life and how we can all renew our lives in the face of unbearable sorrow.

"This is a message of hope...a message that you will heal with time. Well, heal somewhat. I do not think we ever truly 'heal.' We never get over the death of our child, especially an only child as in my case.

Time helps. Your child still lives in your heart, in your memory. With time, you start living another life, a different life...a life not as a parent but a life as a spouse, as a family member, as a friend, and as a career person.

The possibilities are so wide...you can sponsor charities in the name of your child and have his/her memory relived through other people's lives. You can give of your own person to assist people in distress. After what happened to us, we understand hardship, and we feel compassion. We are capable of reaching out.

There is no use dwelling forever upon one's grief. We have to live with the living. My daughter, Valerie, was 16 when she died. She has now been dead longer than she lived. To this day, I still miss her dearly and think of her every day, several times a day. In the course of these years, I have volunteered for several charities: the UNICEF shop, the Florence Nightingale Foundation, and programs that take care of the elderly. I also became the Godmother of several children in third world countries. How rewarding to be able to help those young people get a decent start in life.

Sometimes I have the feeling that Valerie is helping me in my everyday life. Of course, there is always the supreme reward: the hope of seeing my child again in the afterlife. What a soothing, enlightening perspective. Be positive. It helps."

Editor's note: my friend sponsored a 4-year-old girl in Chile with letters and money and helped her finance her nursing schooling. The girl is now over 23-years-old, a registered nurse and works for the Armada de Chile, Chilean Navy. Francine also had the pleasure of visiting and meeting her for the first time a few years ago. She is so proud of this child's great success story. Other children Francine has sponsored were from the Philippines, Guatemala and India. If you want to make a difference as has Francine, the cost of supporting a child is $30 a month through the CFCA at www.cfcausa.org.

Part 2

Coping With Special Days of the Year

One of the hardest parts of trying to live day to day after the death of our child is the question, "What are we going to do when the holidays/ special days arrive?" We will feel awkard, as will our family and friends, celebrating these days knowing the stress we are going through. All these special days stab at our heart when they arrive, since we once shared them with the child we lost. These informative articles discuss what others and I have personally done to get through these celebrations to look towards the future with hope.

Death leaves a heartache no one can heal,
love leaves a memory no one can steal.
- from an Irish headstone

1.   *Getting Through the Holidays*

After losing a child, most of us find the holidays challenging. Try some of these suggestions to give new meaning and purpose to your lives.

LET OTHERS KNOW HOW YOU FEEL. Giving others the tools they need to help you through the holidays is a precious gift, and loved ones and friends will appreciate knowing how they can be of help and what you need from them. You, in turn, will benefit from these caring individuals.

PLAN. Spend that special day with people you enjoy being with rather than staying at home thinking of the past. Consider taking a short trip over the holiday, perhaps a 3-4 day cruise can be enjoyable. Alternatively, go to a beach location, completely opposite of usual holiday weather. There is no way to escape grief and all the reminders of the holidays, such as songs played on the radio, the sounds of laughter, or the smell of a turkey or ham cooking. However, one needs to relieve the anxiety that comes this time of year. Spending the holidays where you feel nurtured, emotionally safe and comfortable is a good idea.

SEND NOTES or cards that you have bought, written or had printed to special friends, including thoughts about your child or a fond memory you have that includes that person, their children and your child.

DONATE your time or your money to a school or organization your child enjoyed or perhaps help at a hospital where needed. There are people out there who can use our help during the holidays, particularly care homes for the elderly, and it is a good way to be a friend. Caring about others adds purpose to our lives.

DECORATE a tree, a room, a fireplace with mementos of your child that you, your friends, and loved ones can look at and discuss with them. They, in turn, will probably be able to contribute a memory of your child.

HELP OTHER PARENTS WHO HAVE LOST A CHILD. Invite them to your home on a special day and share good memories of both your child and theirs. We all have a special bond with parents who have gone through the same kind of loss. We understand so well.

KNOW YOUR LIMITATIONS. Grief is all-consuming. When the holidays arrive, added stress places demands on your time and emotions. Do not do too much. Try to do what is best for you at that specific time. Accommodate your current needs.

ACCEPT HELP WHEN NEEDED. Sometimes the holidays are overwhelming and you need others to help you with decorating, cooking and shopping. Those close to you are probably trying to offer support at this time. Allow them to, and you will both feel better.

BE YOURSELF. If you want to cry, then do. If you want to laugh, do not feel guilty. You are not obligated to do anything you do not feel like doing. Grieving is nature's way of healing the mind and heart from the worst loss of all. This holiday is for you to begin to open your heart to the new you.

CHANGE TRADITIONS. Sometimes a different project for the holidays will make the season more bearable. Some traditions may be a comfort, while others might cause pain. For example, you may want to set up your Christmas tree with memories of your child on it in pictures, while you may not want to invite relatives over for Christmas dinner and listen to all the stories of other children's activities. Consider which traditions to keep and which traditions to let go of this year. Do not feel like you have to do something because you have always done it.

USE A SUPPORT SYSTEM. Having someone to talk to and share your feelings with is an excellent way to get through the holidays. Not only do you need friends and relatives during times of grief but there is also a great variety of support groups everywhere. Call hospitals, churches, hospice and community centers, Compassionate Friends or Bereaved Parents USA to find a group that suits you. Meeting others in the same situation as you can develop understanding and friendships that may last a lifetime. No one else understands like another bereaved person.

TAKE CARE OF YOURSELF. It is often difficult for those who have experienced a loss to sleep, eat, exercise or rest but remember to drink lots of water. It is important to do all of these to function on a day-to-day basis. If you feel you cannot handle all this, there is nothing wrong with talking to and seeking help from a medical provider.

YOU WILL SURVIVE THE HOLIDAYS AND BEYOND. Above all, remember that you are a survivor and will make it through the holidays and continue with your life and the things that matter most to you. This time of year is probably the most difficult during your grief journey, but you can get through it. The best gift you can give anyone you love, even someone you have lost, is being true to yourself and living your life to the fullest.

2.   *New Year's Resolutions*

Each year on January 1, I say to myself, "What do I hope to accomplish this year that I haven't done yet or want to continue to do?" This year it will be to continue writing, continue speaking to bereaved parents at conferences and to help my hometown bereavement group continue helping those on their grief journey. I encourage you to ask yourself what you can do this year for yourself and in memory of your child. It will not change what has happened to you, but it will give you a purpose and add great meaning to your life. It has to mine. Here are some thoughts for you to ponder.

I will
- try to use my inner resources to cope with my loss either alone or with another loved one helping me. In the process, I will remember that this is a long journey and not to worry that in my upward journey, I may fall but will have the strength to get up again and continue.
- take care of my body with exercise, sleep and eating right, because if I do not, my body will revolt. I must save my energy and use it wisely. I will not create an artificial front of pretending because of my loss but express my feelings as I work through my child's death to the best of my ability.
- remember that I did the very best parenting for my child, that my child knew it and that she loved me as much as I loved her.
- use external resources when I feel hopeless or in need of help and not feel ashamed about it.

- not expect everyone to understand and will try to be patient with those who do not.
- try to be happy about something at some time during every day so that eventually it will come naturally.
- reach out and try to help someone else in pain, knowing it will also help me.
- talk about my child always whether others feel uncomfortable or not. My child was the most important person in my life and I do not want to forget him/her.
- fight my way back to a meaningful life once again. That is what my child would have wanted for me.

I hope this will be your best year since losing your child and that each year will get better and better.

3.   *Memories at Thanksgiving*

Thanksgiving: a time for families to gather around the dining room table, a time to share the story of the pilgrims and their bountiful harvest, a time for caring, a time for loving.

Thanksgiving 1993 was the last time I saw my daughter in a family-type setting, so it is hard for me to think of it as a joyous occasion when it comes around every year. I still miss her laughter, her stories, her hardy appetite, as I would watch her gobble down the turkey she loved so much. That last time she was just married a little over a month, so she drove from California to Arizona that weekend with her husband, planning to spend Thanksgiving with the family and her friends still living in the area. I remember how uncomfortable she was in the trundle bed. She complained it was hard to be close when the two beds were not really connected. "After all," she said, "they were officially a married couple and wanted to sleep close together!" I laughed and told her she could deal with it for a few days, that there would be so much time, so many years together. No, it was not to be. It was only a few months as it turned out.

I do not think it matters that she was my only child. I am sure it is just as hard for parents who still have other children, to look at that empty seat at the dinner table and remember, with love, other happier Thanksgivings. We all do the best we can.

One year I helped at St. Vincent de Paul dining room for the homeless. I stood behind the counter and dished out food. As they came through the line, I played a game with myself. Let us see if I could guess the situation and why these people were homeless, why they had no one with whom to share this holiday. What had happened in their lives to place them there on that day? As hard as I tried, I could not imagine. Then I heard some stories...illnesses, lost jobs, deaths...all heartbreaking to say the least. You always think your situation is the worst, until you hear another's story.

It is then I realize how lucky I am to have people who care about me, people who invite me every year to their dinner table, those who know it is hard for me but want me to know they understand. Those people are my true friends. I try as hard as I can to enjoy myself. Sometimes it works well, other times, not so well. I believe that is to be expected, and when it's over, I breathe a sigh of relief that I don't have to think about this particular holiday for another 365 days.

A father, who is in my first grief book, had to deal not only with the loss of his child but also with the fact that no one wanted to talk about his son anymore. Father and son were on a helicopter sightseeing tour of New York City, when the helicopter malfunctioned and crashed into the East River. The father tried desperately to save his son by continually diving beneath the water, but to no avail. His son got tangled in the wreckage and was the only one of four people to drown. It took this father many years of therapy and help from friends and grief organizations to sort out his devastation. In time, he recovered but in the process became estranged from some family members and friends who wouldn't talk about what had happened.

He has and will always have fond memories of many Thanksgivings that included his son, and he likes to bring these memories up during the dinner parties he and his wife have during the holiday season. On the other hand, the relatives who he still talks to are not interested in discussing his child.

He made a conscious decision: at the dinner table when everyone is talking, he brings his son's name into the conversation. "They don't have a choice," he says. "I make them listen. I do not want my boy forgotten, so I talk about the good memories. What else can they do, get up from the table and walk in the other room! Maybe, just maybe, one time soon, they'll remember how important it is to me and include him in their conversations both at the dinner table and other times of the year."

We all want others to remember our children. I, for one, am glad he does that. He is making a point. Just because his child is not here physically, he existed; he was important; he had dreams for the future; he wanted to make a difference; and he is loved and will always be.

Our love for our children will never leave us; they will always be a part of us. Love and memories never die.

4. Mother's Day History and Remembrances

For a mother who has lost a child, it is undoubtedly one of the worst days of the year. Your child is no longer here to celebrate with you. While most celebrate the joys of parenthood, grieving parents often feel a special anguish. In particular, the mother who has lost her only child may believe she is no longer a mother since her only child has died. Because your child died does not take away that title from you. Rest assured that although your child may not be here on earth with you, you will always be a mother and you should celebrate this holiday, if you can, as you would if your child were alive.

I recently read a brief history of Mother's Day as well as getting information on the two women who created it, Julia Ward Howe and Anna Jarvis. Here is some background information.

Julia Ward Howe, writer of The Battle Hymn of the Republic, was the first to conceptualize the first North American Mother's Day in the late 1800's. Julia was distraught by the death of so many sons of so many mothers during the War that she called for a mother's day celebrating peace and motherhood. This lasted approximately 10 years.

Julia Ward Howe was the first to conceptualize Mother's Day in the late 1800's.

It planted the seed for Anna Jarvis to establish the first official Mother's Day celebration in 1908. Anna never married nor had children of her own. She devoted herself to establishing a national Mother's Day as a way of honoring her beloved mother who died during that time. In Anna's view, her mother deserved a memorial because she had lived selflessly and endured considerable suffering… seven of her eleven children had died in early childhood. According to historians, Anna's mother mourned the deaths of her children throughout her life.

Anna insisted that the holiday always fall on a Sunday so that it would retain its spiritual moorings. Because of her efforts, President Woodrow Wilson in 1914 finally proclaimed the second Sunday in May as Mother's Day. Although Anna could not prevent the new holiday from quickly becoming a marketing phenomenon, she did try. Speaking out against the mire of commercialization that threatened to engulf Mother's Day, Anna attempted to preserve her creation as a true holy day, a time for solemn reflection and prayer. She was arrested and put into jail several times. As with most holidays during the year: Christmas, Easter and Thanksgiving, sometimes we forget the true meaning behind them and Anna didn't want that to happen. When she died, 40 countries were celebrating Mother's Day and now it has spread throughout the world, albeit very commercialized.

Mother's Day was borne of a daughter's grief and love. More importantly, it is intended as a tribute to a bereaved mother…a brave woman who lost multiple children, but who managed to live with an abiding kindness and generosity toward others. Many women today continue to have meaningful lives in the face of unthinkable loss.

Mother's Day symbolizes both the joy and the vulnerability inherent in parenthood. From the moment a child is born, hope and the possibility of tragedy go hand in hand. Anna's mother understood the fragility of life.

For Anna, Mother's Day was a time for quiet reflection and the sharing of cherished memories. I believe that is what the day means to all bereaved parents.

There are no words to describe what I feel every Mother's Day. To those of you who have lost a child, you know exactly how I feel. The hole in my heart will never heal. Friends try to do a little mending and it helps, but it is one of the saddest days of the year for me, and there is no getting around that fact.

Some thoughts on Mother's Day: Many years ago, I was so proud when Mother's Day luncheon in my sorority approached, and I could invite not only my daughter, but also my mother and mother-in-law to join me. Four of us would show up, the most of any sorority member. Everyone seemed envious. Two years later, I was the only one of the four of us left. I never knew whether that was the reason the event was dropped from the sorority calendar or whether it was because some of the girls did not have anyone to bring. For me it was the best thing. I cannot imagine how I would have felt attending with no one at my side. More than likely I would not have gone.

I also remember that first Mother's Day after Marcy died. I wondered if anyone would remember I was a mother and will always be a mother. Yes, I did get a few cards from Marcy's friends and my friends, and that put a smile on my face. After a couple of years, most of that ended except for two special people. Life goes on and others forget and move on, but not for bereaved mothers.

That first Mother's Day after Marcy died, I wondered if anyone would remember I was a mother and always would be.

The first few years after Marcy died I was invited to Mother's Day brunches with family members. That eventually ended also. Through the years, I have had friends invite me out on that day, but I mostly want to forget what day it is.

On a happier note, my husband, who is not Marcy's father, is always so thoughtful and says so many kind words on that day and throughout the year. He lets me know he understands my pain. He tries to empathize as much as he can even though he only knows Marcy through pictures and video. They never met.

This past Mother's Day I was on a Europe trip. I lost track of the days and dates and had to be reminded what day it was. I could hear and sense those traveling with me being very careful of what they said, and they didn't discuss their children at all for fear it would hurt me. Their kindness is always appreciated.

On Mother's Day we all need to do whatever makes us happy, whatever gives us some joy or whatever feels right. That could be a trip, exercising, taking a walk or just staying at home. Giving ourselves permission to grieve in our own way is very healing and very helpful during this difficult time.

> *In your gathering of memories,*
> *invite your courage to remember*
> *everything*
> *Sascha*

5. *What You Can Do on Valentine's Day*

Valentine's Day, a day for love, a day to celebrate with those you love. Valentine's Day, another holiday to remember your child, who can no longer celebrate with you. It is a difficult day for all of us who grieve the loss of our child or children.

So I say, embrace Valentine's Day as a special day to commemorate your child and celebrate your love for him or her. Death may end our child's life, but it does not end the relationship we had and still have. Death does not sever bonds of love, and the love we shared with our child will never die either.

What can we do to celebrate this day? I am a writer and what better thing to do but **write** about my child. I can do a poem, an anecdote, a letter, a song, or a story about something memorable she did for me on Valentine's Day.

My daughter never forgot to give me a card. Nor did she ever let her Dad forget. She then had to check out not only the card he bought but also the gift as well. A stamp of approval meant we could all go out for dinner to celebrate. I wish I had kept all the cards she gave me. I only have a few. Usually they were cute cards with a touch of humor, while her father's cards were more on the romantic side. **Give a card** now to a niece, a godchild, a good friend or your grandmother. Remembering others during holidays is a kind thing to do.

Another thing you can do is to **go on a short trip** to a special location you both loved. I remember one year Valentine's Day fell on a weekend, so we all went to romantic Sedona, AZ, to celebrate with Marcy and her boyfriend at the time. I have gone back to Sedona on special occasions and immerse myself in the healing power of remembrance.

This Valentine's Day, **light a special candle** for your child. Perhaps do it every Valentine's Day and continue that tradition as you remember the good times you shared. Make it a holiday where you decide since it is February and Arbor Day is close, why not **plant a tree** at your child's school this year and why not every year.

Talk about your child to anyone who will listen. You will find that people do care and do remember him or her. They may even contribute to the conversation as to something they, too, remember about the child. It will not only surprise you but also please you as well that your child is not forgotten. Recently, I had that experience, and it makes my day every time.

Volunteer some time to an organization that could use your help. Do it in honor of your child. It could be a child-related organization, a pet organization (if your child had special pets), or any local hospice group. Doing something good for others can help ease your pain.

If you work in an office, show your thoughtfulness to colleagues by cooking a nice dish and bringing it. If cooking is not one of your strengths, buy a Valentine cake to share. There is nothing wrong with celebrating the occasion with those whom you work with all year long. It can also **strengthen your workplace relationships.**

For those who work for you like the newspaper boy, your doctor, your house cleaner, or the mail carrier, present each of them who are visible on that day, with a small **token gift** like a white rose or a little chocolate box. The smile you get in return will make the gesture worthwhile

Finally, be creative on this day and **make a Valentine's Day craft**, like your child used to do for you. It can be a home decoration item for the rest of your family to enjoy or even given as a gift for a loved one. Use materials easily available around the house.

My wish for all of you on this holiday is that you always have wonderful memories, accented with a smile, a laugh or a giggle, of your child who cannot be with you physically on this day but will always be with you in your heart.

6. *Father's Day Reactions*

Father's Day is your day, Dad, and I hope you celebrate it with loved ones. Many fathers react differently to this day depending on where they are in their lives, especially a bereaved father.

One bereaved father from a TCF chapter in Tampa, FL, wrote this poem:

As this day approaches, I wonder how I will react.
Am I still a father?
I will sit quietly never allowing family and friends to see how I feel.
I will miss my son, but I can't allow myself to "break."
I must remain strong and always be the "rock."
I wish I could just let someone know how much I miss my little angel.
How much I cry and how much I miss hearing "Dad, I love you."
I am a father, but I wonder, will I just pretend, that it doesn't bother me?
Remember me, for I hurt, too, on this special day.

Another father says it took him many years to accept the death of his child, but he has now moved on. "When my daughter was alive, she, with the help of my wife, made a big deal about Father's Day, always serving me breakfast in bed, giving me a little gift and spending quality time with me. Knowing and understanding how I feel, my wife continues to make it a special day. One of the things we do is visit her grave and tell her what we did that day. At home we light a candle in her memory."

Gerry Hunt from a Compassionate Friends chapter wrote, "Every father believes in his role as protector of his family. He is assigned the job of fixer and problem solver. He is told since his youngest days that he must be strong...and must not cry. But each father among us has had to face that point where no amount of fixing, problem solving, and protecting has been able to stop their child's death."

Father's Day is often a forgotten holiday, overshadowed by the longer standing tribute to mothers. For the bereaved father, it is a poignant reminder of the bittersweet memory of a loved, now lost, child; bitter for the death, pain and recognition of the inability to stop what happened. Fathers do not often have a chance to share their hurts and concerns. Oftentimes they are unable to do so.

As for my own experience, it was after midnight before I got up the courage to call Marcy's father, Jess, to tell him his only child was dead. It had taken me a while to digest it myself, but I knew it only fair that he also know, even though we were divorced.

I heard his sharp intake of breath and the words, "Oh, my God, no" when I said those words I never thought I would have to hear myself. I asked him to make all the arrangements and call me in the morning. He did as I asked and by morning, we knew all the plans. He was functioning on a different level. He was plunging himself into a task so as not to think that his whole world had been shattered. He was numb...it was not real.

In his own words: Jess's reaction: *When reality set in, I began to cry and to this day, when thinking about Marcy and alone in my house or my car, the tears form. I always tried to be like my father, successful but not show emotions. I held back many emotions, particularly at the beginning of my grief period. I think that's how I got through the funeral and the eulogy I gave. When a relative sent me a note saying that I was so courageous for giving that eulogy, I felt special.*

At first, I had a hard time focusing on tasks. I couldn't concentrate for long periods of time. I learned at a grief support group that what was happening to me was normal. It was a relief to know I wasn't crazy. Others talked at these sessions about tasks they had done before their child's death that they could no longer do. It took me months before I could go back to work for a full day.

After Marcy's death, everything pleasurable about getting old was gone. My child, who I was very proud of, would no longer be able to do successful things. I would no longer get the pleasure of her excitement hearing of her adventures in her job. The fact that there is no one to carry on the family name or traditions haunts me. I'm sure Marcy knew how much I loved her although I frustrated her at times with my ways, such as taking days to return her phone call.

The heartache that comes when the natural order of things change (your child dying before you) is unfathomable. When I hear news about a child who dies from whatever cause, I cry. I cry for the child, but I also cry for the parents who are left behind to live with this tragedy for the rest of their lives.

I did see a psychologist for a while who was of great help to me, and although this may sound trite, the passing of time itself is a great help. You do eventually heal to a certain degree, but you never forget.

In my life now, when I am at a gathering, I always try to tell what I call a Marcy story whenever appropriate, something she did or said that I remember that will bring a smile or a laugh to people. That way she is always with me in good memories. Sometimes I cry and sometimes tears just form, but it makes me feel good to talk about her. And I know it's a healthy thing to do even though the pain will never leave me."

Perhaps this Father's Day should be a time when family members, whoever they are, give Dad a hug, do something special, help with the chores, and most of all, let him know how important, needed and loved he is.

7. *New Holiday Traditions*

Make paper ornaments related to child
Watch old videos of your child
Help out at senior homes
Make hospital visits with gifts
Raise money at charity events

When we lose our child, we change. We are now different people from when our child was alive. The rituals that we once held sacred to do with our children during the holiday season may no longer be important or appropriate. Old traditions sometimes bring more pain than comfort. We can look towards making new rituals and new beginnings with our family and friends. Here are a few suggestions for your holiday celebrations, no matter what your beliefs.

If your family has always decorated the home with beautiful ornaments each year, perhaps a new tradition of having family and friends make a paper ornament for you that represents something related to your child. For example, if your child was active in soccer, perhaps a soccer ball with his name written on it. If your child was in choir, perhaps some paper musical notes or musical score sheets. If he or she liked a special food, cut something out from a food magazine and place on an original ornament made out of any product handmade or bought. You will end up celebrating your child's life and he/she will be remembered. You can keep them or try a different theme every year that somehow relates to your child. It does not take the pain away but will warm your heart. You may also find out something new about your child that you can treasure forever. Whether Christian, Jewish or any other religion, it does not have to be on a tree. It can just be a collection displayed during the entire holiday season.

Invite friends and family to watch old videos so they can see your child's personality show through. This will also provide an opportunity for everyone to talk about your child, and each person will feel more comfortable doing it in this setting, as will you.

Helping others during the holiday season is a good way to share yourself and may give you an opportunity to share stories of your child with others. You can help at a senior citizen home, a hospital, a food bank or a soup kitchen feeding the hungry. Any of these choices will allow you to feel good about yourself and that you are doing something in memory of your child.

Go to the children's ward of a hospital and bring something to give related to what your child would have wanted or something you have treasured with which you can now part. It could be a stuffed animal, a game, jewelry or some clothing. Whatever it is, you will make a new friend and feel that your item has made a difference to a child. If you feel up to helping out at the hospital in addition to just visiting, hospitals can always use volunteers. Give of yourself and you will have a better holiday.

Different charities usually hold events during the holiday season to raise money for the following year. If, for example, your child died of a particular illness, try to participate in that event in any way you can. Give a donation if you feel you cannot do anything else now, or you can actively help to set up booths, sell food, or anything else that needs volunteers. Many charities have something like a walk-a-thon, for example. Not only is walking a healthy activity, but also you may meet new friends by participating and be able to share your story with them. Other organizations may hold auctions or raffles, and if you are good at getting items to raffle or auction off, perhaps that can be a new tradition for you.

Try to enjoy the holidays by creating new traditions. The pain of losing your child will still be there, but in doing for yourself and others, a little ray of sunlight will shine through the clouds.

Part 3

Informational Techniques
To Cope With Grief

Twenty articles dealing with volunteering, how to start a support group in your town, writing condolence letters, worldwide candle lighting, attending bereavement conferences and inspirational music for the bereaved are just a few of the topics discussed in this section. Taking care of other aspects of grief outside of the personal coping journey is just as important for bereaved parents to come to terms with, learn about and accept.

*In three words I can sum up everything
I've learned about life. It goes on.*

- Robert Frost

1. Finding Organizations for Volunteering

After the death of our child and an initial grieving period has passed, we may ask ourselves, "What can I do to be helpful to others? What can I do to make another person's life worth living? What can I do to make a difference while adding meaning to my own life?" You may have a need to channel your pain, as well as your time and energy you once devoted to your child. By reaching out to others, you may feel useful once again. Here are some thoughts on volunteering for all ages and in many situations. As you look into this further, you will find there are many other areas besides the ones I list for you.

Homes for senior citizens can always use volunteers to help older adults get around, eat a meal, run errands or just offer support by talking to them. No experience is required to do those things. Older adults would probably love to hear stories about your child, your situation and your life. You, in turn, can ask them about their life. It is an opportunity to do some good in your community, to make new friends, and to share your life and loss with them. You may also be able to offer valuable information and support because of what you have gone through and they, in turn, may be able to communicate and empathize with you. Contact the city officials or look up senior residences in your phone book and call.

Children's hospitals in every state are always asking volunteers to help care for, play with, change diapers, or sit with young children who need support as they go through therapy. I always thought after my daughter died this would be what I would do with my free time. A friend of mine, who lost her son, wanted to hold the sick babies and comfort them when she retired. Neither one of us fulfilled our dreams and thoughts, but not because we did not want to. Life got in the way as I trudged through the grief journey, and I am now busy writing and working part-time. My friend helps one of her children in her therapy practice most of the week by doing the accounting. Our lives are useful in other directions, but helping at a children's hospital remains in both our thoughts. My daughter had tons of stuffed animals, in fact a whole room full of them, and I would like, one day when I can let go, to take some of them to a children's hospital or organization and distribute to others. That is still on my bucket list. SAFE (Stuffed Animals for Emergencies) is one organization that collects donations and distributes new and almost new stuffed animals, toys, books and blankets to children in hospitals and shelters. They find the animals "ease the children's nerves and calm their fears," according to the organization.

Hospice and palliative care volunteers can provide home care breaks for caregivers and visits with patients as well as make the final days for a patient restful and comfortable. Dementia care volunteers, who are interested in working with these very special patients and families, get additional training. Bereavement calls to caregivers to support them through this difficult time and offer additional information and resources is available as is simple filing, data entry, and other general clerical duties at the agency's offices.

Make a Wish Foundation is a valuable asset in kid's lives. When there is not a cure, there is still something positive in their lives to look forward to, according to one social worker. A wish experience is frequently a source of inspiration for children undergoing difficult medical treatments and a positive force that helps them overcome their obstacles. Volunteering can be a few hours each month or a few days each year…whenever you can make the time. The Foundation offers volunteer positions in the areas of committee member, event/fundraiser planning, language translators, office help, public speaking and wish granting.

Humane Societies entice animal lovers. In most states, volunteers should have compassion for homeless animals, a commitment to create a brighter future for the animals and a consistency and reliability in helping care for the animals. If you are able to give a minimum of 8 hours per month for at least 6 months, two primary ways are available for you to volunteer. First is to help screen potential adopters, walk the dogs, play with cats and help in the thrift store. Secondly, you can open your home to needy animals on a foster care provision, allowing the animal time for healing to prepare for adoption. Animals do not take the place of humans, but they are a great source of comfort to many who have had a loss of some kind.

Feeding America volunteers hope to end hunger in America. The network feeds over 25 million each year. Volunteers can help in local communities through tutoring kids at the local Kids Café, repackaging donated food for use at food pantries, transporting food to charitable agencies or clerical work at the various offices. Contact a local food bank to point you in the right direction.

A Caring Hand, the Billy Esposito Foundation in the New York City area has a mission "to met bereaved children and families wherever they are in their grief and fulfill their needs in a caring and knowledgeable environment through services to help them with their emotional journey and give financial assistance to aid in future education." Volunteers are vital to creating a safe and welcoming place and invited to contact them throughout the year. They ask for a one-year commitment to co-facilitate group sessions after 12 hours of training. They also need help for various short-term projects throughout the year from stuffing envelopes and answering phones to doing outreach in the community. Attempt to find a similar organization in your state.

Other information on volunteering is on web sites both locally and nationally. Look them up on Google:

- FEMA
- Network for Good
- Online Volunteering Service
- September 11 National Day of Service
- Volunteer Match: Where Volunteering Begins
- Halfway houses
- Drug rehabilitation centers
- Meals on wheels
- Schools

- Shelters for battered women and children
- Neighborhood Watch
- Youth organizations
- Museums and art galleries
- Libraries and churches
- Community theaters

In a quiet moment ask yourself: What skills do I have or can learn that can benefit others? What causes are important to me? Give voice to your heart through volunteering. When you become a volunteer, you can make a positive difference where you live in the lives of others. Best of all, your child would be very proud of you.

2.   Giving Eulogies

When a good friend of mine died, I felt a great desire to stand up at her funeral and give a eulogy about her. No one asked me to do it, but I felt a great need for everyone there to know what my friend was really like, as I saw her through my eyes. I sat down at the computer and stared at the blank page. What could I say about her that was personal for me, that made her personality stand out, and that might make people say, "I didn't realize she was like that...."

I must have sat for almost an hour. Did I not know this person well enough? Was I being foolish trying to do something I was not capable of nor had ever done before? Suddenly it came to me. I would tell a few anecdotes about what we enjoyed doing together, some of her quirky ideas and thoughts we would discuss, and her personality, how we met, our interactions with one another. It all came flooding out. There were funny incidents, humorous personality traits, how weird she sometimes acted. I had more than enough to write about because it came from my heart.

I was lucky, writing about someone I knew. If asked to give a eulogy about someone you did not know well at all, that is a much more difficult task. Here is the way I would go about it:

I would ask friends and relatives stories about this person, some of the things they liked to do, what they were like as children, what type of education they had, what they liked to eat, drink, read, sing, who they liked to quote, and what activities they were involved in. Were they a fun person, quiet or just a character at heart? Was the reason a sudden death, an act of violence, suicide or a long illness that took this person? These are all the things one should consider when conveying your sentiments.

You may be surprised at all the information you can gather. Writing a speech about this person may not be the chore you dread, but a way to convey to those who knew this friend how much he or she will be missed. Remember, those at the funeral want to remember their friend with comforting words and the appropriate tribute they believe this person deserved. No one expects perfection at a time like this...writing from the heart will more than accomplish your goal.

Finding the right words is sometimes a chore. Books like *Do Not Stand at My Grave and Weep* can provide numerous suggestions, poems and quotes to use. Online sites with help include www.webcrawler. com, www.speech-writers.com/eulogy, www.eulogyspeeches.net, www.messages-of-sympathy.best-price.com and www.pronto.com.

After my experience with writing my first eulogy, I hope that I have done a service by honoring my friend and for those attending the funeral. I feel good about the whole experience and would probably do it again now that I understand how to go about it.

3. Starting a Support Group in Your Town

I would encourage anyone who needs the help of a support group to deal with the death of a child to start their own, if there is none in the area in which you live. The group does not need to be part of a national group of bereaved parents. It can serve any purpose you need in your own area of the country.

In order to get started the local newspaper should be contacted to see if they will do a story in the paper about your first and subsequent meetings. Place flyers in hospitals, funeral homes and religious institutions. Local hospice groups in each state can help. Contact one of the national bereavement organizations for any information or encouragement to get started. See what happens and whom you meet. It can be the beginning of a new life with new meaning to it.

Through the encouragement of another bereaved parent, I brought 17 bereaved parents together in my community, both mothers and fathers, who have specifically lost their only child or all their children. I hope that through these parents we will get others. We now have a place to talk about our children and share fond memories, laugh, enjoy a cup of coffee and discuss coping techniques. We are all in different stages of the grief journey, from a few months to over 15 years. Our children were all different ages when they died. The causes of deaths range from car accidents and illnesses to drug overdoses and suicide. We feel comfortable sharing and enjoy each other's company.

The group you start does not have to be for only childless parents. You can combine forces for a meeting and then break up into smaller groups within the meeting, such as: childless and those with surviving children. You can have groups by the number of years the child is gone: 1-5 years, 6-10 years, and over 10 years. There are many ways of running these groups, and I encourage you to try to put one together.

Everyone going through the grief process should know that it eventually becomes bearable. You do not heal from grief. It is with you your entire life. You can live with it; it becomes a softer grief. You will eventually find something useful and suitable to do with your life and in doing so will honor your child's life.

Many people in my book *I Have No Intention of Saying Good-bye* talk about what they have done to remember their child or children. It is comforting for them to tell their story; it is heartwarming for me to write about them. They are brave parents. They have accomplished a lot since their child died and they have made a difference. I hope that everyone going through this unbearable loss will one day make a difference. That is when you will know you are on the other side of grief. These support groups can start you in that direction.

4.   *Dealing with Wrongful Deaths*

Below is some information related to the topic of wrongful deaths that may be of value to you or someone you know. I would encourage anyone involved with this or who knows someone who is, to check with a lawyer before pursuing anything legally. Each state has different interpretations of the laws.

A wrongful death refers to a lawsuit that claims a victim died due to an individual, company or entity's misdeed and carelessness. The victim's survivors are entitled to monetary damages because of improper conduct or negligence. A wrongful death claim could result from one of the following: auto, motorcycle, airplane, helicopter or boating accident; a medical malpractice resulting in decedent's death; criminal behavior, occupational exposure to hazardous conditions or substances; or a death caused by negligence during a supervised activity.

Ron Goldman's suit of O.J. Simpson for the death of his son is an example of this. Although he won the case, he has never seen one penny of the compensation he was awarded.

I know of one mother whose son died while in military training, not in enemy combat. The irony was that this boy was willing to give his life for his country by being in the military in combat, but this is not what happened. According to his parents, the death was unnecessary and happened through carelessness. Without going into detail, the parents chose to pursue legal means due to their son's death. Not all those involved choose this route, but these parents did as did Ron Goldman.

Dealing with a tragic or sudden death is very difficult. You may not even be able to deal with it right away, but it is best if you can get evidence in a reasonable time, if the case is going to be pursued. A skilled lawyer can help collect evidence, give legal tips or advice, complete all necessary legal documents and built a case against the opposing party. Those involved should clarify the lawyer's payment system and how and when updates will be given on the progress of the case.

Parents and surviving family members such as a wife or children may be entitled to receive compensation from an insurance company or from those held accountable for the death. Even though no amount of money will compensate for the loss, receiving compensation may somehow soften the grief.

Medical, hospital, funeral expenses, pain and suffering are the most common areas that you see compensation given. Different states have different statutes and laws to follow. Check that out carefully.

As the military parents said, they would have preferred not to have to deal with it at all, but in their son's memory, they felt they had to do something. In their grief, they also sought out TAPS, a grief support group for those who had a loved one die in the military. TAPS helps them deal with their loss emotionally, they told me. "We couldn't have made it through without them," they said. Seeking professional help for the emotional aspect is as important as seeking legal help.

If you feel you want to pursue a case of wrongful death, read everything you can about the topic and find a good attorney to lead you on the right path.

5.   Taking Care of
Funeral Planning

No one wants to think about death and dying, but in general, I believe it a good idea to do some funeral planning.

There are many funeral planning guides out there (google it), but here are a few simple suggestions for everyone.

We cannot plan our lives with the thought that we are invincible. Planning avoids incurring financial hardships with funeral expenses. Funerals are not cheap, but with careful planning, you can eliminate much of the emotional pain as well as the monetary one.

There are between 50-90 separate decisions to make when planning a funeral. Some of these decisions are

- Where to bury the loved one
- What type of casket
- What type of flowers
- Who can come
- An after ceremony get together
- Make a list for reference

By doing it all in advance, every detail can be discussed and the price of every item can be explained and paid for in advance or over a period of time, so there are no financial burdensome surprises with which to deal.

Most of us would be too busy grieving to be able to think about these things. I remember when Marcy died, I could not think; I did not want to think. I knew I could not do the planning. I knew nothing about planning a funeral for any loved one. When my dad died long before, my mother did everything. When my mom died a year and a half before Marcy, my step-dad did everything.

When Marcy died suddenly, she had made comments to a good friend the week before as they were attending another funeral that she thought it was ridiculous to have a service at a place of worship and then a procession to the grave for another service. "For me, I want just a grave-side service." Since she had never said anything to me, (it was something never discussed at her age), I was stunned to learn that information, but decided to follow her wishes. Who would have ever thought it would be so soon after that casual request to her friend. We only did a graveside service and then had friends and family over afterwards for coffee and a bite to eat.

Pre-planning also allows more freedom and creativity for the funeral service. As an example, friends of Marcy's spoke and recited words to a song they thought appropriate. At some funerals, singing can be heard, balloons released, and flowers displayed for loved ones. Families of the deceased usually include in the obituary or in the funeral program where others can send contributions to honor the deceased. Choosing a casket and type of casket are as important as the obituary written. Some individuals choose to write their own if they know they do not have long to live. If a loved one has to write it under emotional duress, it is even harder.

Talking to loved ones, understanding their desires, and following their wishes will help everyone during this emotional time. Death is never welcome in any home, but preplanning a funeral takes some of the sting away.

6. *Angel of Hope Memorial and Worldwide Candle Lighting*

Many states have an Angel of Hope Memorial, giving all bereaved families the opportunity to memorialize the loss of their child. The statue is a dove-winged angel, whose face is that of a child's, its arms raised as a child to be lifted. In its wings is hope.

Richard Paul Evans' book, The Christmas Box, was the impetus for this memorial. The story is of a woman who mourns the loss of her child at the base of an Angel Monument. Because of this story, the Angel Monument was introduced to the public and is now known worldwide as the Christmas Box Angel. Although Evans' book is mostly fiction, the Angel Monument once existed in Salt Lake City. Speculation says that a flood destroyed the original statue. Evans commissioned a new Angel statue in response to reports that grieving parents were actually seeking out the Angel as a place to mourn and heal. At its dedication in Salt Lake City, there was no division in race, in religion, or in class. Just one heart huddled together for shelter from life's storms to find peace and hope at the base of the Angel.

This statue has provided comfort and solace to thousands of parents since 1995 and many cities now have their own Angel statues due to the diligence and dedication of bereaved parents who have made it happen through donations. There are opportunities for donors to receive recognition on a wall as well as a plaque for their loved one in many of these locations. If your city does not have an Angel of Hope, perhaps it is a project you can work on and make it happen in your area.

Each year, a worldwide candle lighting for all children who have died is held on the second Sunday in December at 7 p.m. Many communities have these at the site of the Angel. Others plan the ceremony at a local park, church or cemetery area. To find out more about the ceremonies, contact The Compassionate Friends (TCF) website at http://www.compassionatefriends.org/.

It took many years of hard work to get legislation to make this an official event. The U.S. Senate unanimously passed the resolution declaring this day National Children's Memorial Day. It allows us to join in unity to remember and honor the memories of all children who have died.

The worldwide candle lighting creates a virtual 24-hour wave of light as it moves from time zone to time zone. Hundreds of formal candle lighting events held, as well as thousands of informal ones conducted in homes as families gather in quiet remembrance. It is believed to be the largest mass candle lighting on the globe.

Patricia Loder, executive director of The Compassionate Friends (TCF), says that this event shows that people from around the world can gather in peace and unity to remember all of the precious children who have died. This is TCF's gift to the bereavement world and Pat says they are so happy that it has received such universal acceptance.

Visit the Worldwide Candle lighting page on TCF's national website where there is a brochure with helpful suggestions on how to plan one of these services if none is available in your area. Call the national office of TCF toll free at 877-969-0010 for information and suggestions for where there is a service in your area. In addition, you may leave a heartfelt message on TCF's online Remembrance Book opened only on that day.

Each year I attend one of the Children's Memorial Day Services at a local mortuary. More and more parents are becoming aware of its existence.

I remember it looked like almost 1,000 people that attended on one cold December night. A variety of people read poems, favorite sayings and said prayers. We all filed past the Angel of Hope as music played, and then given white flowers to place at its base or into its arms. As we made our way back to our seats, we each received a candle, which we lit. We were also given a very soft, cuddly teddy bear to hold on to (and keep) as the names of each child were read who were either buried in that cemetery or whose relatives had bought a plaque near the Angel honoring their child.

I could hear sniffling, sobbing and soft talking all around me. I could also see the anguish on the stunned faces of the parents who, in their wildest imagination, never dreamed they would be sitting here with the rest of us. Parents were of all ethnic, cultural and religious affiliations. We were one in that hour that we honored and remembered our children.

Many allied organizations joined in the remembrance such as POMC, MISS, MADD and BPUSA. Participation was high: funeral homes, churches, hospice and local bereavement groups, as well as informal groups meeting in many communities.

This ceremony is a powerful message to the world. Would it not be even more powerful if we could get everyone once a year on this special day to light a candle for all children who have died? I hope that this year you will be able to participate in some way on this memorable day.

7.   Writing Condolence Letters

Whether you are a bereaved parent or just know of someone who has lost a child, the most challenging letter an individual writes is a letter of condolence, particularly one about a child. The written word can bring much comfort when coping with a loss. We want to convey so much to these bereaved parents, particularly if we are close to them, but how to go about it can be difficult.

Many people send pre-printed condolence cards from any card store, but making the effort to compose an original handwritten sympathy message is more likely to be appreciated, especially if you know the person well that is receiving it. A relative or close friend who values your relationship will do the latter, although at this point any recognition is good.

A few tips on what to say follow. First, acknowledge the loss. Say how shocked and dismayed you were to hear about the child dying. Then express your sympathy and let the grieving person know how much you care or perhaps you can relate to the anguish of their loss if you, too, have been there. Talk about the child and some personality traits, qualities or an anecdote that evoked a smile, a laugh and a fond memory. Perhaps that child influenced your life in some way or did something that you will never forget.

<u>**Tips on What To Say in a Condolence Letter**</u>
Acknowledge the loss
Express your sympathy
Talk about the child
Offer to help around the house
Close with a caring thought

Offer to help with the little things the parents find difficult at the beginning, like shopping, running errands, answering the phone and taking care of the other children. Finally, close with a caring thought, like "My thoughts are with you at this time," "You are in my thoughts and prayers" or "We share in your grief and send you our love."

If you think you need help in writing a condolence letter, search online or visit a bookstore where you will find many sources to help you complete the job. One such book's title is *Words to the Rescue*. Check Google.com and type in "writing sympathy messages" and many sites will come up that you can explore. Whatever you find, make sure it will only guide you, not write it for you. Your note needs to be personalized and come from the heart.

I have had to write many of these letters over the years and can sometimes be at a loss for what to say. No two children are alike; no two deaths are alike. The words do come, sometimes spilling out as my heart goes out to these parents. I feel good when I finish and send the note. I always have to hope, though, that these parents understand my words and wishes, and that I have not waited too long or written it too soon. Bereaved parents also have to understand that a condolence letter to them is done out of caring and love and should be accepted as one way for others to express how much the child meant to them also.

On a personal note, I received and cherished many beautiful letters when Marcy died and even learned a lot about my daughter through these condolence thoughts that I never knew before. I learned how much Marcy cared for others, how she always went out of her way to help others, what a good friend she was and how much her friends and family love her. I have kept them all. I could actually say these letters changed my life. They gave me the impetus for putting together a small booklet of these letters to give to people who I knew would appreciate receiving them. Their gracious comments led me on a long road to write my first grief book, including thoughts and some of those letters in the book and wanting to share additional stories of hope from others across the U.S.

Planning my life around my daughter was not to be. One never knows where life may lead you, but in doing what comes from the heart, only good can come of it. My plan is to live my life to the fullest, always keeping Marcy close to my heart and involved in everything I do. If writing a condolence letter can help a grieving parent in some way to know their child's life was important to others like me, then I have accomplished something very meaningful for the bereaved parent and myself.

8. *Attending Bereavement Conferences*

Do yourself a favor and attend a National Bereavement Conference during the summer months or even just a regional conference during the year, given by many national bereavement groups. The largest one is The Compassionate Friends Conference usually held in July in different parts of the United States each year. The conference helps all those who have lost a child. In addition, grandparents and siblings can attend. The other national conferences include Bereaved Parents U.S.A. and Parents of Murdered Children (POMC), not as big as TCF, but with the same goals. Parents come together to not only remember their children but also to talk about different issues they confront on a daily basis.

I choose to attend Compassionate Friends each year where they hold sessions dealing with all facets of child loss during these three-day conferences. Over the years, I have found them to be helpful, give good information and deal very well with helping others tackle the grief journey. People from all occupations come to seek help whether it has been one month, one year, 10 years or longer. Wherever you are in your journey, there is a place for you at these conferences.

There are around 100 different types of workshops for different needs, enough of a variety to please everyone under any circumstance, in addition to well-known keynote speakers on the topics. I usually give a few childless sessions. Over 100 sessions are available for those with surviving children such as grief stress, multiple loss, sudden death, moving from loss to legacy, what to do with a child's belongings, marriage and communication after a child's death, organ donation, healthy and unhealthy grief, signs from our children, anger and guilt, humor in grief and scrapbooking, to name a few.

Sharing sessions at night, where parents get in a large circle and discuss their situation is probably the most popular time. Only there can you shed your mask and be yourself, cry, laugh or do whatever you need to do as you tell your own story while others listen attentively.

On display throughout the lobby of the conference areas are boards and boards of children's pictures labeled with poems or some information about them...beautiful children from infancy to adults who died far too young, some of whom would never know marriage and children of their own. It was hard to believe these beautiful children were all gone and that some families had lost more than one child.

The crying, the laughter, the squeals of delight at seeing long time friends from other conferences kept assaulting my ears, but it was seeing the hugs (much longer than a normal hug) of both men and women who understood what the others were feeling that touched me deeply. In some cases, I was one of those people.

Because I speak at this conference does not mean I have stopped grieving. I will always grieve for my child. Most of the time it is hard to get through any speech I give without tears forming, especially when mentioning her name. It is a normal reaction that does not embarrass me. I believe I will always reveal that part of me. I do want others to understand I still hurt feeling the greatest loss of all in my heart and mind. I have moved on and this is what I choose to do.

I have met many new friends at these yearly conferences, friends I feel comfortable talking to, listening to and even giving suggestions to. I have seen bereaved parents walk into the conference with no hope and come out smiling with a new reason to live after having attended many of the workshops and listening to nationally known speakers. I have seen first-hand the miracles that come out of these conferences.

One of the good outcomes is of a father, who for years, would not believe that anything would help ease the pain over losing his daughter. His wife had tried for years to get him to go to a conference. She understood its power. This one year she had succeeded. After the

3-day conference at the closing ceremony, he turned to her smiling, took her hand and said, "I promise to always trust your judgment from now on. I love you." She smiled, knowing he had finally turned the corner. She never asked what happened. She thinks the sharing session where he broke down and was able to get his feelings out helped. She was relieved to know they could both move on together from that point on.

There are over 600 chapters of The Compassionate Friends around the country and more than one in most states. Bereaved Parents U.S.A. and Parents of Murdered Children have many chapters across the country with meetings you can attend locally and national conferences similar to TCF. Regional meetings are on a smaller scale but try to produce the same results. Alive Alone tries to hold a conference every few years. Contact them for further information for parents who have lost their only child or all their children.

Parents travel many miles once or twice a month to attend local meetings of these chapters. They want to be with people who understand what they are going through, and there is no one who does more than another bereaved parent.

9. *Starting a Foundation in Child's Memory*

I have finally found the one thing to do in memory of my daughter that has made me feel complete. In the past, I bought stones and bricks in her memory at many new buildings in town and plaques in strategic locations. A drama building in a summer camp, built from her friend's contributions, has a dedication plaque to her. Even though these were all wonderful, I felt as though something was missing, something that could go on for many generations and something from which others could benefit.

What I found was a foundation that I could give money to in order to benefit those who want an education to pursue their dreams. The foundation is named in memory of my daughter and is for the benefit of those pursuing careers in the communication or drama fields of interest, something that Marcy could not fulfill in her short lifetime.

Foundations benefit those students who need financial help to pursue their dreams and they do not have to pay back the money.

Those persons interested for either academic or financial reasons will be able to apply to the foundation, and with input and contributions from Marcy's father and myself, we will decide the recipients for as long as either one of us is alive. Also included in this foundation fund, as beneficiaries, will be active theater groups who need monetary help.

There are many ways and many areas of interest so those starting the foundation can see where their monies are spent, and they can specify whatever is of interest to them. This particular area of interest, communications and drama, is what we chose, since it was a big part of who Marcy was.

Money can be put into this foundation during my lifetime by myself, by Marcy's dad, by relatives or by friends and then after my passing, the foundation will be completely funded through a clause in my will and hopefully last for many additional years. It is being started during my lifetime so that I can see the beginnings of the benefits to others and even have a say in who gets the money. It will be like setting up a scholarship.

A person does not have to be rich to help others. On the contrary, whatever donations are made in the pursuit of benefiting others is a worthwhile endeavor, no matter how much it is.

Helping others has always been a goal of mine, and I believe Marcy felt the same way. She would be happy to know what I am doing in her memory for future generations. It is a good feeling and one that may interest others, hence my reason for mentioning it. These foundations can be found in most cities, and I encourage others to look into this. Financial and tax advisors are privy to much of this information and can help find what best suits your own circumstances.

May it bring you some kind of peace to know that your child will not be forgotten and that you have taken a horrible tragedy and made something positive out of it.

10. Giving Another Person a Chance at Life

Thanks to a cornea transplant, Jason was able to see again for the first time in 31 years; at the age of 39, a kidney transplant saved David's life; for Richard, a bone marrow transplant meant the chance to live a normal life again; and when Darcy's son gets older, she will tell him about the kidney transplant that saved her life. All of these are examples of people who received organ donations.

In my first book, one of the stories I wrote about is the death of two children in the same family from a car accident and the donation of the organs of the daughter to help others live. "She was such a loving child, we were certain she would want her organs donated to help others," said her parents. They believe that one or two children may be alive today because of their donation, and they feel good about that. Although always a difficult decision, it was the right choice for them. Others have a right to feel differently. The information I provide here is for those who, by their wills, on their driver's licenses, or though conversations with loved ones, choose to make that same life-altering decision to help others.

A few facts: over 79,000 U.S. patients are currently waiting for an organ transplant; nearly 3,000 new patients are added to the waiting list each month. Every day, 16 to 17 people die while waiting for a transplant of a vital organ such as a heart, liver, kidney, pancreas, lung or healthy bone marrow. Nearly 10 percent of the patients currently waiting for liver transplants are young people under 18 years of age.

Organ, eye and tissue transplants offer patients a new chance at healthy, productive, normal lives. Acceptable organ donors can range in age from newborn to 65 years or more.

The organization, Donate Life America, founded in 1992, is a not-for-profit alliance of national organizations and local coalitions across the U.S. dedicated to inspiring all people to save and enhance lives through their donations. They publish brochures, program kits and other materials, and provide technical assistance and referral services. Contact this group or make your wishes known to a hospital, your health care provider or a lawyer.

A study a few years ago showed that while 91% of adults support the idea of organ donation, only one in three is aware of the proper steps for committing to become a donor, as procedures differ from state to state.

I encourage you to look into organ donation. You can change someone's world by being a donor. It is the ultimate charitable act.

11. *The Divorce Rate*

Like many myths, the divorce rate following the death of a child has snowballed way out of proportion. Harriet Schiff in 1977 (The Bereaved Parent) said that as high as 90 percent of all bereaved couples are in serious marital difficulty within months after the death of their child. She does not cite her source for this, and no one ever questioned her about it. Therefore, it became fact. However, it is not true, and grief experts challenged the myth. By 1998, they said there was no evidence of higher divorce rates among bereaved parents.

In 2006 The Compassionate Friends commissioned a survey, and one of the questions dealt with divorce. They found that only 16 percent of parents divorce after the death of a child and only 4 percent said it was because of the death…that there were problems in the marriage way before the child died.

One parent said, "It's been three months (August, 2008) since the loss of my second son and only remaining child. He was 27 years old. My oldest son died in a car accident in 2001. I've been alarmed at the incredible strain my marriage is under

---

Only 16 percent of parents divorce after the death of a child; only 4 percent said it was because of the death, that there were problems in the marriage before the child died.

---

since my daughter-in-law and 2-year-old grandson are now living with us. My husband is my son's stepfather and is grieving in his own way. I hope to find some ways of coping and am encouraged to know the myth behind the high divorce rate among bereaved parents."

This is not to say that there are not lots of problems when a child dies. One of the biggest is that husbands and wives grieve differently. One may want to attend a support group, the other doesn't. One couple in my first grief book had a tough time with that but found that as long as they talked about their child together and kept the lines of communication open, that commonality saved their marriage and they both grew from it.

Another couple said, "We became a divorce statistic because we could never bridge the hurt we inflicted on each other after our daughter died. It was never that we did not love each other. But the hurt was too much to ever let us come together again."

How a child dies can cause friction in a marriage. If parents start blaming each other for the child's death, whether it is from anger or just misplaced blame, that can lead to marital stress and in turn, divorce. Couples have to make a commitment to want to stay together and get support from a therapist, a support group or close friends they trust.

"I truly love my significant other, but it is really becoming difficult because our grieving process differs so greatly that is it definitely putting a huge strain on our relationship," said one mom. "I am trying my best to hold on. We go for counseling, and I hope that will help us."

Against all odds, many couples have found that their marriage grew stronger after the death of their child. They learned new coping techniques and they had a great desire to move on with their lives while never forgetting their child.

One couple who suffered the loss of their son at age 39 was afraid of becoming another statistic because of the strain on their marriage, but she and her husband remain devoted to each other.

A parent said that when you are both drowning, you both have to cling to the same thing in order not to push away from each other in the storm of grief. "We clung, and still do cling, to God. He was our buoy in the hurricane, and He is the only reason we are making it."

A mother who lost her 13-year-old daughter to unknown causes said, "I can't believe the divorce rate after such a horrendous event can be at such a low percentage. For two people trying not to drown in their individual sorrows, it is a near impossibility to find the strength to offer a hand to help the other. Those who say they've come through the battle with an even closer relationship are very blessed."

And finally, a mother said, "It's true that when you are both drowning you can't be each other's life preserver; that is why it is important not to depend on your bereaved spouse as your major and certainly not your only source of support for a long time. If you each give each other time and space to grieve in whatever way is helpful for that individual, and you draw strength from those that have it to give to you, you CAN take that strength and plow it back into your marriage, and ultimately support your spouse. The number one thing you can do to protect your marriage is to draw strength from whatever sources will sustain you and take care of yourself, so that you are the nurturing and supportive partner you want your spouse to be. We know. We have been there and have survived the storm."

Find the way to what is best for both of you. My best advice is not to rely on any statistics you read or hear but to follow your own heart and know that most marriages can survive the loss of a child if the partners are willing to try to hold it together by whatever means they need to.

Note: Each parent I interviewed in this article requested to remain anonymous.

12. *Finding Your Child on Google*

A few days ago, I started rummaging through the internet and decided to put in my daughter's full name when unmarried and see what came up. I was astonished to find two google pages of information on her and links to me, my book, open to hope and the fund established in her name. She died in 1994, and yet, I now have proof that she still lives on for others to see and read about.

The most interesting note I saw dealt with her high school alma mater. Back in 2004, ten years after her death, two of her friends (and I recognized the names, since I knew most of their names during her high school time) had written a brief note saying how much she is missed and mentioned what I assume was the topic of two funny incident between all of them.

Wow! I can't tell you how good that made me feel. I now know I am not the only one who remembers. So many sites and ways are available to remember our children and find information about them. Nothing is sacred these days.

I had a comment about Marcy's high school and perhaps doing a scholarship there on a blog I wrote. It was an anonymous note but here was someone else who knew Marcy who had a suggestion for keeping her memory alive 15 years after her death. As a side note: for many years, I did do a scholarship where I taught. Now I am concentrating more on her foundation and helping others through that means.

I also found information on her grade school graduation list from 1980. In addition, the 1985 University of Arizona yearbook had her information. Once in 1979 she made a political contribution and even that was still on the internet! I googled Marcy's married name, and the same information came up. Amazing what we can find and do on the internet.

I encourage all of you to google your child's name and see what comes up. I hope you find that many other people remember your child.

13. Celebrating a Loved One's Life Through Art

Celebrating the uniqueness of a loved one who has died has healing capacity beyond words, according to Adrienne Crowther, who started a memorial art business a little over a year ago. Her mission was to help people honor and memorialize their loved ones forever with art.

"I have a lifelong passion for art, and I believe that it's really the ultimate expression of who we are as humans. Art can express emotion beyond words," she said.

Ironically, for Adrienne, her husband recently died, and she and her children were able to put their beliefs to practice. Both of her daughters are artists and they designed and built a cremation urn for the dad. The design came from their hearts and carved by hand, reflecting his personality and essence.

Shine On Brightly, the name of her business, features artist-designed, hand-crafted products to memorialize and celebrate lives of loved ones. A variety of materials and styles are available, including ceramics, jewelry, glass, wood, metal, textile art and paper art pieces. The website www.shineonbrightly.com also offers links to valuable resources to help with end-of-life issues. It also shows in pictures some of the beautiful artwork that they can do.

Shine On Brightly is also responding to the rapidly growing rate of cremations in the U.S. and worldwide. Container options for cremation remains are limited and are often mass-produced outside of the U.S. Adrienne said that many people are commissioning art pieces to incorporate the ashes of a loved one.

"We also offer beautiful objects to honor that person in other ways for those who are uncomfortable with keeping the ashes. For those clients we have customized books, jewelry and textile pieces."

At the web site, one can select a product or work with one of their artists to create a unique, personalized memorial. "Art can pay tribute to someone and serve as a constant symbol of the unique spirit within," she said. "We believe that our products are a wonderful way to memorialize a life."

14. Two Singers Perform Inspirational Music for Bereaved

When I hear a particular song that my daughter enjoyed listening to, singing to or dancing to, my heart skips a beat and emotions rush to the surface. It is a poignant moment and tears may come to my eyes, or I may have a smile on my face, remembering those times. Two singers who sing and write inspirational music for the bereaved are Judy Philbin and Alan Pedersen. There are also many others.

Judy Philbin, who sings inspirational music, has a CD called *Candle In the Window* with songs and words most bereaved parents can relate to. Her soft melodious voice is easy to listen to, as the words speak to the heart. In this CD she explores the many levels of "saying goodbye" while affirming that love never dies. Some of the song titles include: *"You Are There," "Cry You a Waterfall," "Really Gonna Miss You," "Love Survives,"* and *"I Still Can't Say Goodbye."*

Judy realized the powerful way in which melody and lyrics can offer solace and healing following the death of a loved one. Her music helps one let go of emotions that may be bottled up inside and enables others to move on in their grief journey.

Judy has been singing for grief support events for 20 years in addition to other venues. After losing her daughter during pregnancy, it was the hospital support team that helped her understand there are many ways to help others. For her, it was music.

She realized her songs and words were changing people's lives. "Parents would say to me, 'Your voice is healing' or 'That one song helped me understand what I am going through,' so I compiled songs into this CD knowing this is my way of helping others," she added.

Judy's collection of songs takes the listener deep inside to places that may not otherwise be accessible. Each song honors the memory of a loved one while celebrating the power of love to transcend the boundaries of death. To get a copy of her CD or to listen to the tunes, go to www.candleinthewind.net or iTunes.

Alan Pedersen, bereaved father and award winning songwriter, successful recording artist and nationally recognized speaker on grief and loss, began his journey in August of 2001 when his only daughter Ashley died in an automobile accident.

The tragedy took his life in a direction he never imagined. His pain and journey toward finding joy again have been the subject matter for three highly acclaimed CDs of original songs.

As an in-demand keynote speaker and workshop presenter, Alan is featured at many international, national and regional conferences including The World Gathering on Bereavement, Compassionate Friends National Conference and the National Gathering of Bereaved Parents U.S.A.

His music is used at hundreds of candle lighting services, balloon and butterfly releases and by hundreds of professionals and organizations as a healing tool for the bereaved.

"We were put on this earth to love our children for as long as we live, not for as long as they lived." He believes that healing comes slowly, but does come as we reach out to others who share this journey and offer our hand to help.

Alan is available for bookings and his gentle mix of humor and straight-from-the-heart talk wrapped around powerful songs about love and loss make for a unique, healing and memorable concert experience.

His goal is to reach out to the smallest and most rural of grief organizations throughout the United States regardless of the size of the concert. It is a special journey he is calling Angels Across the USA Tour. Those who know Alan know this work has always been a ministry to him; he now wants to expand that part of the outreach. For additional information on Alan, go to www.everashleymusic.com.

On a personal note: I, too, realized from the beginning that songs with meaningful words would be part of my life. Many songs remind me of my daughter for one reason or another. One of the last songs she spoke of before she died was the theme song from Whitney Houston's, *The Bodyguard*, "I'll Always Love You." It is not that the words fit Marcy perfectly. It is just that she loved the song, so now I love it also and always think of her when I hear it on the radio or on my *Bodyguard* CD.

A John Lennon song *"Woman"* is on a video that one of Marcy's friends made showing highlights of her life. When that song plays on the radio, I always think of the videotape and how meaningful the words are to me now.

One of Marcy's friends had a special song played at her funeral that she thought fit Marcy's personality and life perfectly. The song was *"Some Fantastic Place"* by Squeeze. When I heard it, I agreed completely. There are many key words in the song that I could identify with Marcy: tenderness, friendship, love, smiling, humility, and beauty.

I now listen to songs with a new perspective and try to share my thoughts on them with others.

15. Anne Frank's Father Inspires Others

Most parents want to have their children remembered, want to talk about their children and want others to know them as they knew them.

One such father and now famous daughter is Otto Frank and his daughter Anne. The Jewish family fled to Amsterdam, Holland, at the start of WWII, lived there until one day they either had to go into hiding or be sent to concentration camps. They chose hiding and lived in the annex of Otto Frank's office building for two years before betrayed. All went to concentration camps, but only Anne's father survived. Anne died a month before liberation. After returning to Holland, Otto Frank received Anne's diary that friends found and kept during the time they were imprisoned.

After reading the innermost thoughts and feelings of Anne from ideas and beliefs on happiness, courage, giving, goodness, freedom and usefulness, he realized there was much he did not know or understand about her, particularly under the circumstances they lived.

In spite of everything, I believe that people are good at heart...
Anne Frank

Anne senses she was a good writer and says in one writing during confinement, "The nicest part of my diary is being able to write down all my thoughts and feelings; otherwise, I'd absolutely suffocate!" During the hiding period, Anne does not only write in her diary, she also writes short stories, some of which she reads aloud to the others in the hiding place.

Initially, Otto Frank feels uncertain about the idea but he finally decides to fulfill his daughter's wish to devote herself to human rights and to achieve mutual respect for one another through her writings.

He does this by sharing her gift of writing and wisdom with the world and devoting the rest of his life to human rights. The book, *The Diary of Anne Frank* is now the second most read book in the world next to the bible and translated into many languages.

For the fourth time I toured the Anne Frank House in Amsterdam, Holland, recently. The stairs and the hidden bookcase leading to the secret rooms used by the Frank family are still in place, as are some pictures on the walls. It is both an emotionally moving and educational journey to go there, but, most importantly, it is the story of a parent who lost a child and did not want his child or her intelligent thoughts forgotten.

I, too, feel this way, as I am sure most parents do who have lost children. I now have a book that includes my daughter's story and her thoughts and feelings. Although it is written from the parent's perspective, not the child's, it was just as important for me to tell my story as it was for Otto Frank to let the world learn about Anne during her confinement.

I have set up memorials, foundations and remembrances for my daughter, Marcy, as Otto Frank has for his daughter Anne. Parents may differ in the feelings they have about letting personal writings become public if a child has died, but one thing is certain: building some type of memorial for your child whether they become famous or not will help them to live on in your heart and in others' hearts forever.

The traveling Anne Frank exhibit shows in many cities throughout the world besides Amsterdam. Adults find the exhibit personal and touching. Student teen groups are challenged to ask questions such as "choices made", "helping" and "persecution" when looking at the Frank family's story. Working with teaching aids specifically developed for high school students that include historic pictures and a concise timeline, they learn about Anne Frank in addition to what happened during the Second World War and the persecution of the Jews. The program can be adapted for different levels and age ranges.

Otto Frank, more than likely, never dreamed what the release of Anne's diary would mean to others, nor did he envision its thought provoking effect on the world in general. I am sure he was very proud of his daughter. He died in 1980 in his nineties.

To read more about Anne Frank go to www.annefrank.org. You can learn about the various memorials and foundations started by Otto Frank and even place a leaf on Anne's tree, the one she was able to see from the attic window looking towards the sky.

16. *Organization That Helps Families Cope*

If your family has suffered the death of a child, and both remaining children and parents need support dealing with the pain and the grief journey, an organization called NEW SONG, started in the Phoenix, AZ, area provides nurturing support for grieving children and their families.

It also offers comprehensive grief education for volunteers and professionals and is hoping to be nationally recognized as a model grief support and training program whose purpose is to restore hope to children and those who love them. Volunteers undergo over 25 hours of classroom and 20 hours of mentor-led training to facilitate, under the direction of professional staff.

This non-profit, non-denominational organization started in 1990 and provides the following services: support groups for grieving children ages five through 18 and their families; referrals to other community agencies; and child-specific grief training for

---

New Song Center helps adults learn how to support and parent their grieving children as well as help themselves.

---

volunteers; and education for caregivers, mental health professionals, clergy and the community at large. Support for the program comes from individual donations, foundations, organizations, businesses, churches and synagogues.

Because a child's response to death is different from an adult's, New Song Center focuses on the unique needs of children and their families in grief. While children are supported through art and play techniques, New Song Center helps adults learn how to support and parent their grieving children as well as help themselves. Each family learns how to work through their pain, share memories and go on living without the loved one who died.

My friend, Sandra Howlett, a bereavement specialist for Hansen's Mortuary in Phoenix and speaker for Hospice, has been involved with this organization since 2003. She says the children are divided into separate groups: ages 5-7, 8-10, 11-12 and teens. Parents and caregivers (grandparents, aunts and uncles) are in a separate group as are young adults from 18-26 who come on their own. There is an orientation program, which the whole family comes to, and then they divide into groups. They are also required to come to one monthly program where they do family projects.

An evening at New Song would go like this: you would arrive at 6:30 p.m., have pizza all together (It's always pizza, Sandra says), hear announcements and then divide up into respective groups for an hour or so. The group then comes back together, lights a candle in honor or memory of those who died, sings a few songs and finally gets in a circle to say good-bye for the evening. The groups meet twice a month from August to the end of June, a 10-month period each year.

Sandra explained that age specific exercises take place during the meeting time periods geared at accepting experiences, feelings, memories and playing out things using art, music, puppetry, journaling and discussions. With the adults, it is having a place to talk and discussing what it's like being a parent in a grieving home.

After a death in the family, adults are sometimes too involved in their own personal grief to respond adequately to the needs of a child. The family unit is thrown into turmoil. Because children deal with powerful emotions differently from adults, their grief may go unrecognized. Their depression, fear, guilt and anger may be acted out and labeled as behavioral problems in the home and school, instead seeing it for what it is, a reaction to the death of a loved one.

With New Song, a child is your ticket in and that child needs to be at least 5 years old. If you are an adult with no children, you cannot come. It is a family dynamic organization.

"When a family leaves New Song, they are not the same family as when they first came," she told me. "It can take many years, depending on the type of death. As time moves on you progress to a new level. It is a special time when you find a moment you can smile and appreciate the sunlight and not feel guilty about it."

I hope that this organization will be the inspiration for similar organizations forming throughout the U.S. to help not only bereaved parents but also the entire family.

17. What Must Be Organized After a Death

It is inconceivable to imagine all that one has to do when an older child or any close family relative dies.

I watch others struggle through papers, through household items, through jewelry and artwork and through the money situation. I know exactly what they are going through. I have lived through the death of both of my parents, my stepdad and my daughter Marcy. I am at a point in my life where I can tell you that no matter how many times you must deal with death and its emotional journey afterwards, it is never easy.

For those who may want to keep a list for future reference, here is what I would do to make the beginning of your grief journey…the technical part of the death…easier to handle.

Planning is necessary. Do what you can call an "Estate Planning Document" for every member of your immediate family. You can be almost any age to have one of these. It is not only for adults. By doing this document, you are creating a record of trusted advisors, the location of your important documents and other important information needed after a death. Include the following in this planning document: a list of where all important papers like a will and trust are located, insurance policies, house and auto information, names of lawyers, where you keep your money and stocks, and who to contact just in case something unexpected takes a loved one. Write down all your passwords and where all your keys are. Pick out where and whom you would like to do funeral arrangements.

You may even want to pick out family grave plots. Put this information in a safe place. The more you can do, the easier it will be for those left behind. Contact a lawyer if you need help with this, but for your own health and well-being, get it done early in life. Those of us who have been through this understand how your life can change in one split second.

By doing an estate-planning document, you are creating a record of trusted advisors, the location of your important documents and other information you need after a death.

When Marcy died, I wanted to contact all her friends to tell them of her untimely, sudden death. Fortunately, we had been close, so I knew most of them. The rest I found in her address book. That was the easy part. I had already purchased family plots so I knew where I would bury her. Her important papers I found at her home, some in file drawers, some things on the computer. Because she did not do one of these estate-planning documents, to this day, I do not know where some things are and may never know. This is one reason I feel so strongly that this is an important exercise to do.

One of the hardest parts of any death is to dispose of the personal items. When I received most of Marcy's things sent to me, I kept the important items. That included most of the jewelry, some clothing I knew I could wear, all the awards and trophies she had won in high school and before, stuffed animals, photo albums, papers from her workplace and beautiful items she had bought on her travels.

I knew that others wanted things to remember her by, so I then went through the other items and some of her jewelry and asked her friends what was important to them. In some cases, they asked me, and I was happy to oblige where possible. I remember one friend asking for a dress, another asking for a neon light she had given Marcy and still another friend asking for Venetian Glassware that matched her own that she and Marcy had bought while traveling in Italy. The first two were no problem. The last I couldn't do. I hope her friend understood.

I did go through all the albums and offer pictures to others, throwing out the ones that had no meaning to me, selling some of her clothing, and giving away a few stuffed animals, but saving most of them for my Godchildren and even me! I love stuffed animals; they are very comforting to hold, particularly when you are having a bad day.

The entire process is not an easy one but necessary when a loved one dies. Make it easier on yourself and other family members by being prepared to handle all situations that may come up.

18. *Music/slide Project To Honor Child*

A special project I did in memory of my daughter was a slide/music show on the computer. This is something you may want to do. You can look at it anytime, when the memories overwhelm you, or when friends and relatives come over who would appreciate seeing it.

I started out by going through every album I have of my daughter from birth to death and chose the pictures I thought represented her life through candid action shots of activities she was involved in, trips she took, boyfriends she had, honors she won, and of course, family posed pictures. I wanted the pictures to have her laughing, smiling and sometimes serious…as she was.

Seeing all those pictures brought back so many good memories of our time together. I limited it down to around 50 photos (a very hard task). This can be adjusted, depending on how long the music is that you choose. You want it to match perfectly and can start with too many and cut as you edit.

Each picture should be on the screen for no more than 5-6 seconds. I think I did a picture every 4 seconds so I could get more in the time space I had. Any less time than that…you'll get a headache trying to see everything in the photos before the next one comes up.

Next, I pondered about the music. Should it be a song she loved? Should it be a song I loved? Should it have lyrics or just be instrumental? Should it be upbeat or slow and meaningful? I ended up choosing "St. Elmo's Fire," an upbeat instrumental song that reminded me of Marcy and seemed to go with all the pictures.

If the pictures were already on the computer, they are all the easier to separate out. If not, I scanned them into the computer. I tried to get them to be around the same size. The face was the most important aspect. Then I placed them in age order. I am not a computer expert, but fortunately, my husband is, so he put together the pictures and music to fit perfectly with a special program he has on his computer. It is a program anyone can purchase and download, or you can have a professional do it for you.

I liked the way it turned out so much that I ended up doing one for my step-dad also and gave a copy to my stepbrother. For this one I used the music Brian's Song, a much softer, gentler type of music that matches the man much better. For a friend we did one similar to Marcy's and used a Josh Groban song. You will know when the music is right for your subject and the pictures you have.

I wish you all luck if you do this project. It is rewarding, and I know you will be happy with the results.

19. Building a Remembrance Website

What better way to honor or remember your child than to build a memorial online. Many good sites offer assistance with the construction of a site and will host it as well. Most are free. On some, there is a small cost, depending on what you want to do. On these sites you can write what you want, put on photos, give background info, talk about special dates and special occasions, show videos of honors won, play songs, display links to special events or have others write remembrances of your child. If this is something you might like to do, choose one of the sites listed for you.

One of the best is the **TCF Atlanta** site: (http://www.tcfatlanta. org). The Compassionate Friends of Atlanta offers free memorial web pages on their beautiful web site. They will provide information and online assistance to you in building a web page for your child. You may have to search for just what you are looking for, but don't get discouraged. It is there and well worth the search.

Loving Memory's homepage (http://www.lovingmemory.net) says, "The loving memory sites have been developed with great care and sensitivity to provide a dignified, lasting memorial to loved ones no longer with us and allows families separated by distance to share and express their feelings." They offer a wide variety of sites including those specifically relating to children. Included in every Loving Memory memorial site is a memorial candle that lights up on the anniversary of the loved one's death.

Memorials Online (http://www.memorialsonline.com) publishes internet memorials celebrating life. They also offer links to grief support to help others cope with their loss.

Ehow: this site (www.ehow.com/how_4812262_memorial-web-site.html) will specifically go through each step to building a memorial site and explain the hosting of the site. According to the site, it helps everyone stay connected in the face of a death.

iLasting (www.iLasting.com) is a memorial web site that offers a basic free setup of 5 photos, 5 stories, 5 candles and 1 song. For a lifetime fee of $135 you can have 100 photos and unlimited stories, candles, videos, and 5 songs including a donation page. It may be worth it to you to spend this one-time fee in order to get a very large memorial site.

MySpaceAfter (www.myspaceafter.com) offers a free service that allows a life journal, photos, videos, songs, and links to events.

Two additional site that are not completely free are (www.virtual-memorials.com) founded in 1996 and hosting thousands, and (www.memory-of.com/public) which can also publish a memory book for your home in addition to hosting a site for you.

Sharing our child with the world is a gift, just as our child was to us.

20. The Difference Between Sadness and Depression

Don't mistake sadness for depression after the death of a child. Many of the symptoms are similar, but depression is a disease and requires treatment and supervision according to Dr. Robert Thompson, family practitioner, bereaved father, and author of *Remembering the Death of a Child*.

"That is an important distinction," he said. "Sadness over the death of a loved one is not a disease. The sad person is usually sad about a particular event, in this case the death of a child. It is a human condition. Sad people are also capable of feeling joy and empathy as well as sadness. The depressed person is very limited in their emotional responses. They feel so bad so much of the time that they really cannot relate to other people and experience any joy or pleasure in their life at all. That is not true of sadness. Sadness stays with us, more or less intense, for our entire life. It is not something we can run away from nor do we want to. Depression usually has a beginning and an end, hopefully. Those are the main differences."

According to Dr. Gloria Horsley, professional therapist, one of the things about sadness is that you don't hear most bereaved people saying they want to kill themselves. They may say they wish they weren't living or they wish they could join the person who died, but that is very different from depression and the idea that they really want to kill themselves.

Ronald Knapp's book *Beyond Endurance* documented this theory in a study that looked at people over a period of six months and one of the characteristics that all families who have suffered through the death of a child have a general desire to follow the child. There were no suicides in his group.

Some therapists can mistake that idea of 'following the child' and not realize it is not a suicidal thought. It is just a thought of wanting to rejoin the person, a natural parental instinct.

I remember thinking when Marcy died that I would gladly have traded places with her. I was almost 50 years old at the time and had lived a majority of my life, a good life, but thought, "Marcy has just begun to live and had so much more to do." I never really contemplated suicide as an answer to my sadness. It never even crossed my mind.

Below are some signs of depression. The ones I have marked can be either sadness or depression, but understand that all of these listed can relate to depression only. I list them so that you will be careful and understand the difference between sadness and depression in your life after the death of a child and deal with it accordingly.

- Difficulty falling asleep or remaining asleep at night (can be either)
- Waking up early in the morning, feeling anxious and irritable
- Marked changed in appetite, either toward overeating or loss of appétit; substantial weight changes (can be either)
- Increased use of sleeping pills, other medications, alcohol or caffeine
- Uncharacteristic short-temperedness, crying or agitation
- Delay or neglect of vital physical needs (can be either)
- Decreased resistance to illness (can be either)
- Loss of energy or fatigue (can be either)
- Subdued mood; expressionless face or flat tone of voice
- Rough handling and other signs of impatience in giving care
- Recurrent thoughts of death or suicide.

Part 4

Personal Coping Strategies to Help the Bereaved

Articles written in this section are from my own personal experiences in hopes of helping all bereaved parents move on and deal with their loss. From remembering my daughter while traveling to special moments in my life that affect my grief journey, the road I travel is filled with both unexpected pleasures and heart-wrenching sad moments. We must learn to deal with all facets of the journey so that we come out on the other side of grief.

To ease another's heartache is to forget one's own.

-Abraham Lincoln

1. Remembering My Daughter in Maui

I love Maui, and so did my daughter Marcy. Her dad and I first brought her there in 1980. She loved the beach, playing in the sand and particularly, picking up shells from the ocean. She continued to visit there.

One time when she was older, we took her boyfriend with us; another time we took her grandmother. We eventually purchased a condominium on the beach to stay in when on the island. Her last trip was with her soon to be husband in 1993. They loved it and vowed to return. It was never to be. She died five months after her wedding in October 1993 in a horrific car accident.

I continue to go and often think of her when I am here...a younger Marcy, running free in the sand and water, lying on the pristine beaches, building sand castles and picking up those seashells she was so fond of.

"Mom," she would shout with excitement. "Just look at this beautiful coral shell. I'm going to take it home and add it to my collection." She did just that and had many unusual ones she was proud of and showed to all her friends. When I go now, I pick up seashells as I walk along the beach. Just as quickly, I return them to the sand, the memories too intense.

On a recent trip, I saw a young dark-haired girl walking towards me...a reminder of Marcy in those tiny bikinis that looked so great on her slim but perfectly curved body. The young laughing girl runs after her dog and into the ocean waters, her brown hair bouncing in the sunlight, her laughter infectious as the currents soak the dog. Barking as an encouragement to follow him, the dog goes deeper, as she calls to him, and reluctantly he returns to the shallow water. From behind the dog, she throws a ball as the dog watches it bounce along the sand and begins to run after it.

I stop short, close my eyes. Emotions overwhelm me, and when I finally open them again, the girl and the dog are far down the beach chasing each other with the ball. They are but a brief reminder of another life, another time, one tucked far down into my heart forever.

We get moments like this any day of the year, any hour and any minute. It is not only a moment in time that seems to take us by surprise, but it can also be a song that reminds us of our child, an anniversary, a birthday, a beautiful sunset, or an activity enjoyed together. Embrace those moments. They are for you alone. You will never forget them nor will you ever forget your child. You never should.

We all have rushes of emotions that can be overwhelming when we least expect it. This does not mean we will not feel better or continue to move forward with our lives. We are different people now than we were when our child was alive. We have different goals; different friends; and eventually, a life with a new richness to it that focuses on what our children left us...the gift of having them.

2.   *The Importance of Time in Our Life*

When a person talks about an important year in his/her life or a news show on TV asks what you were doing when...I always think of my daughter, Marcy's life.

How old was she in 1970 when I first started teaching? What were we doing then? Just a year later, she started school. Years become important in your memory: the year 1966 when she was born, the most important. What was happening in the world then? Viet Nam. President Johnson. The Beatles. Twenty-five cent hamburgers. A friend says, "Do you remember when we..."What year was that?" I ask. "Oh, yes," I finally answer, "I remember that year."

To myself I associate every year between 1966 and 1994 with Marcy. What was she was doing then? If the year is before 1966, it is "before Marcy was born." If I think of the year 1984, yes, that was an important year: Marcy was graduating from high school, and 1988, yes, that too, I remember: Marcy graduated from college and was anxious to start her life in the advertising world. If the year is 1997, yes, that was an important year: I retired from teaching. It was not that important for me, because Marcy was already dead three years by then.

Time has a way of passing very quickly, and we lose track of it. I remember when it was the tenth anniversary of Marcy's death. I wondered how that could be. As far as I was concerned, it had all happened just yesterday...no, today. Today, I felt her body hugging mine as we said goodbye at the airport because, ironically, she had to go to a funeral in California. I felt her strong arms surround me and I thought, "I made this beautiful, intelligent, vivacious woman." What a wonderful life she was going to have! I could never guess it would be the last time I would ever touch her and that a week later she would be dead.

Many years have passed, and I think of all the wonderful things she could have done with her life and new husband of almost five months: children, a life-long career, traveling...she wished and hoped for so much, but it was not to be.

They say time heals. I say time only makes the grief a little softer. It will never, never go away. Time allows you to move forward eventually with your life when you begin to understand you are a survivor of the worst possible thing that can ever happen to you.

3.   *What I Am Grateful For*

As bereaved parents, we might say to ourselves at any time during the year, "What do we have to be grateful for?" Our child is gone from our lives forever. We will never see them again. We will never speak to them again. We will never hear them call out to us again in the night for comfort. We have lost part of ourselves, and when it becomes time for celebrations, we sometimes, for a while, take a step back in our grief journey. I know when any celebration looms ahead, I try very hard not to be negative, but it is difficult.

My daughter's best friend's wedding was the last time I saw my daughter in a formal setting enjoying herself so much as the matron of honor. It was a happy time for us all as I listened to her speech after the luncheon to all in attendance. I try to focus on that and other happy times such as July 4 celebrations, Memorial Day picnics, graduations, getting honors, and Christmas and Chanukah dinners with our friends. I sat down recently and made a list of all the things in my life for which I am grateful. I would like to share that list with you.

I am grateful that

- I could share 27 years of my daughter's life with her. She was a beautiful, intelligent, gracious child who always made me proud. I am so thrilled to have had her, and I would not trade that for anything.
- I have wonderful memories of my child in photos and tapes, in talking and sharing with her good friends, and

in knowing she was loved by not only her Dad and I but also everyone with whom she came in contact.

- Friends are always so willing to share all holidays and important days with my husband and me. Most of the time we go to parties when invited, although it can be very difficult listening to others talk about their children and grandchildren. We go because we know others care enough to invite us, and it warms our heart.
- I have three Godchildren, born from my daughter's best friend. Since I will never have grandchildren, I was honored when asked to be a Godmother as Marcy's Dad was honored to be a Godfather. We are always included in any family gatherings and all birthday parties. The children spend the night occasionally at my home, and we try to do fun things.
- There are beautiful days when the sun shines down, and I can watch the flowers bloom. I wish I could share it with my daughter in person, but I know she is looking down on me and wishing me well.
- I can travel and see all that life has to offer while still around to enjoy it.
- When someone else is in need, I can help, whether it be someone who needs a meal or someone who just needs company so as not to feel lonely.
- I can wake up each day to a new beginning and get excited about the little things I do: exercise, play bridge, work on travel related projects, write and visit with my husband, who is also a very busy person. A fulfilling day is one where I get at least three important things done from a long list of items I would like to accomplish.
- I have a wonderful supportive husband who tries to understand and help me when I feel down.
- I can be supportive to those grieving parents who need help through their grief journey.

Positive thoughts help tremendously throughout the year. Open your heart and mind and allow yourself to see the simple everyday things for which you can be grateful. I hope you can take some of these thoughts and incorporate them into your life.

4. *Birthday Thoughts*

I hate telling people how old I am when my birthday arrives each year. I do not feel old. People tell me that I do not look my age...thank goodness! When Pavarotti died at age 71, I thought, "Yikes, he's not much older than I am." It made me more determined than ever to live my life to the fullest, to do all the things I want to do, to continue traveling, to continue writing, to continue enjoying my friends and to love my husband more and more each day.

I then think of my daughter Marcy, who died much too young at age 27, before she could really experience life to its fullest, before she knew what it was like to have a child, before she could travel the world with her husband and children. I thank God that I had her for 27 years, and she was able to have some wonderful experiences, and that even though she was killed in an auto accident only four months after she married, she at least had a great love and was able to marry.

I hate listening to people who say, "When I retire, I'll travel and do everything I've always dreamed of doing." A great thought, but my philosophy is "Why wait?" Do it while you still can, while you are healthy and can run through the sand, climb that mountain, swim in that sea. Why not go out there and enjoy a beautiful sunset, see all the wonders of the world, write a great American novel, live, live, live...

The grief process can last a lifetime, and these are thoughts that go through my mind. You are always continuing to heal and one of the things that is so helpful is to live your life as your child would have wanted you to do. Everyone must do what is best for him or her in whatever time needed. As time goes on, that grief gets what I call, 'softer.' It will never go away, there will always be a hole in your heart, but you will know when it is time to move on with your life. I have chosen to move on with a great desire to live as long as possible, take care of myself and see everything there is to see and do everything there is to do. I always keep my precious daughter Marcy in my thoughts every step of the way.

Marcy loved to celebrate birthdays. My eyes tear up and the same continuous thought runs through my mind as it always does, "Her death was senseless; what a waste of a beautiful person."

I remember she died the year she was planning a big surprise birthday party for my 50th. I learned that after the accident. I know it would have been great. She was a great planner in all she did. Everything always had to be perfect in what she would do. She was very much like her mother, a perfectionist.

She did give me one surprise birthday party when I was 36 years old, planning and executing it all herself. She was barely a teenager at the time. I remember having to act very surprised when I walked into the house, since one of my friends let it slip out accidentally. She decorated beautifully with balloons and birthday paraphernalia and baked her own cake. As usual, she made sure everyone brought a card and little gift. I remember being surprised at the time that she knew exactly who to ask to the small party and how to make sure I was out of the house for the preparations. Even at that young age, she knew what to do.

Now, many years later, I still think of all the very cute cards she sent me each year. Most of them were very funny and clever. If she lived away from home, I always got a call. She also always made sure her dad bought me something. He used to laugh at how persistent she was that it had to be a special, thoughtful gift. She did not always succeed with him, though, since his thoughts always ran towards kitchenware items. (I did not have that much time to cook since I was teaching full time, so kitchenware was not my favorite. Maybe it was a hint!) She, in turn, always bought her own gift for me; she did not always like what her dad chose.

If her dad wanted to give me a gift a few days early, Marcy absolutely forbid it. "No," she used to tell him. "The gift must be given on the exact date to be meaningful."

I smile when I think of her legacy to me. I always make sure any gifts I give are on the exact date. I try to choose a gift I know the person needs or wants, and I never, never buy kitchenware items!

Thanks, Marcy. You will always be by my side guiding me as I hope I always was for you. I know that somewhere up there you are still wishing me a happy birthday as I do every year for you. I miss you terribly, think of you every day and will continue to do so for the rest of my life.

5. *Memories of the Moon Walk and Happy Times Together*

When we hear the term "moon walk," our minds immediately think of entertainer Michael Jackson and his famous dance that has become a classic. However, there is another literal "moon walk" and in 2009, we celebrated 40 years since man landed and walked on the moon, July 20, 1969. That anniversary brought back a torrent of memories, most of which made me sit in disbelief that so much time has passed so quickly and my life has changed in ways I could never have imagined, both good and bad. When you have lost a child, memories of happy times together can bring a smile to your lips as they do to mine as I remember.

I know where I was at the moment they landed on the moon…my husband, 3-year-old daughter and I had gone to Tucson to visit friends for lunch and sat fixed in front of their television set watching all that was happening: the landing, the first step on the moon's surface. We cheered; we shouted; we knew this would be the start of a great decade. We were so young and innocent as we watched what we thought would be a future of moonwalks and other exciting events in outer space during our lifetime.

However, time has a way of bring us down to reality. Although we had a comfortable life during those years, we didn't make a fortune in the stock market of the 70's and 80's. I did not become a writer for a large newspaper; I taught writing instead and produced my own school newspaper for many years. My husband and I grew apart and divorced. My daughter, who had a wonderful childhood, did not live to fulfill her dreams of having children, a career, traveling or a life with her new husband. All my family members are gone now except for a few cousins; good friends have died needlessly from illnesses or accidents; the world has experienced more wars and terrorism than imaginable.

Seeing the film footage of man landing on the moon again brings me to tears because I think of all the good that could have come from science and technology, yet now we have to worry about threats from foreign countries with nuclear bombs and chemicals that can kill thousands in a second. I think of the days of innocence when we all left our home doors unlocked so friends could come in and visit any time of the day or night. It was okay to let your child play at the park with friends and not have to think about child abductions and worse. I worry about our future children and what kind of world they will be living in.

Of course, I relive my life with my daughter, the great relationship we had, and think of all the wonderful things she accomplished in her short life and how I will always miss her. Since her death, my life has changed considerably. I did eventually do what I wanted: worked for a daily newspaper and wrote books (never dreaming she would be the impetus for one of them). I did lots of traveling, but all the time wishing she could enjoy the trips with me. I had a successful teaching career of 28 years. I have recently met the love of my life and never knew I could be so happy.

I now realize how happy my daughter was with her husband of four short months, looking forward to a bright future. Sometimes I even believe I am living the life she would have, doing the things she would have, meeting new friends and fulfilling dreams I never thought possible. I even find myself using words and phrases that would have come from her mouth. I smile because I know she will always be with me, encouraging me to keep going and doing whatever makes me happy.

Shine on, silvery moon. I may not see the day of moon travel for all of us, but I know, because my daughter lived, I am a better person, and she is smiling down at me from somewhere up there, perhaps sitting very close to that moon.

6.   *Bequests To Give Our Children*

There are two lasting bequests we can give our children:
one is roots, the other is wings.
- Hadding Carter

Roots

I like to think of my time with my child before her death as a nourishing time for her. I am proud of what she was and believe that how her father and I brought her up and steering her in the right direction is what, to this day, makes her memorable to others. Her friends and family always came first. Her thoughtfulness, I always admitted, even exceeded mine.

I remember her wedding and the reception held at a beautiful hotel. First was the cocktail party…but Marcy and her husband were nowhere around. I began to worry when after 45 minutes they appeared, holding hands and a huge smile across their faces.

"Where were you?" I questioned her, a little angry, but certainly curious.

"We stopped in the dining room to make sure everything was okay with the tables, the decorations and the name cards," she said, "and I discovered that they put Dad's table (we were divorced) closer to the head table than yours." "I thought you'd be upset, so I switched the cards. I knew Dad wouldn't care."

"You're right," I laughed. "I probably would have been upset." Cute, I thought to myself.

That followed through with everything she did. Ever thoughtful of others and not wanting to upset anyone, she always made sure that if she had Thanksgiving dinner with me one year, the following year it was with her father. Fair is fair, she would say, and I definitely agreed and had no problem with that.

Another incident made me understand, more than anything did, what made her special. Before she married, she lived with a girlfriend and they had gone out to purchase a lamp for the apartment. Marcy was going to pay for it, but the friend insisted on paying, since Marcy had been letting her stay rent-free until she got a job. Her friend was called a few days later and told she won $1 million dollars from a VISA contest (she had charged the lamp on her VISA). Marcy was so pleased for her.

"I'm curious," I asked my daughter. "Aren't you just a little jealous that she won all that money when the lamp was going to be on your credit card originally?"

"Oh, no," she said. "My friend really needed the money, and I'm glad for her." As I looked at Marcy, I only saw pure happiness for her friend. There was not an ounce of jealousy in her. How proud I was! What a fine human being I brought into this world.

Wings

Let them do whatever they want with their lives. That was always my philosophy. If she wanted to be an actor (at one time that was a possibility), a doctor, an accountant like her father, or just get married and be a homemaker…as long as she was happy, I did not worry about her choices. Where some parents may try to direct their children or worse, tell them what they should do, I was confident Marcy would do the right thing. She was ambitious and wanted a career in addition to a husband and family. I sensed that and let her have her own wings. It was completely her decision as far as I was concerned.

When Marcy was old enough to drive, we bought her a car. We trusted her completely, thought she would make the right choices when appropriate, and, frankly, because she was such a busy woman, were thrilled we would not have to cart her around anymore. She never bragged to her friends about being the first to have a car nor made fun of those who did not have the means to get one. She quietly did what she needed to do and made sure all her friends got to where they needed to, even if a little inconvenienced.

At one point, she announced one day after graduating college that she was going to move to New York to be close to her boyfriend who was going to work there soon in the financial sector. Even though her heart was set on having a career in advertising and to start in Los Angeles, she was a woman in love and willing to follow her man. I did not really approve but, like a good mother, said, "Okay, if that's what you want." At the last moment he changed his mind; she got angry and moved to L.A. without him and got an advertising job her first day there. He ended up following her to L.A., but the relationship never worked out. Why do I remember that so well? Because Marcy bought me a card saying how loved I was by her and wrote at the bottom, "Thanks for letting me make my own decisions and my own mistakes. You're the best mom in the world." I still have that card all these years later.

I choose to believe, and it warms my heart to think, that through these and other examples in Marcy's life, I gave her the needed roots and wings and let her soar.

7. *Gifts of Remembrance*

Sometimes we wonder if others remember our child. I have received so many gifts of remembrances from both Marcy's friends and my friends that I truly believe our children, although gone from us physically, will always have a special place in the hearts of others as well as ours. Encourage others to remember your child. Here are a few stories of what others' stories and comments have meant to me and how they continue to help me cope with my loss.

A First Love

In the midst of everyday living, something special happens that you know you will keep in your heart forever. For me that something special happened recently.

Out of nowhere, I received a letter from Marcy's first high school boyfriend, Dave, from 27 years ago, a very personal letter in which he opened his heart about what Marcy meant to him. Fourteen years is a long time to wait to write such a letter, but just the fact that he sent it at all was so very special to me.

He found me because of an article that appeared in a newspaper about my foundation in Marcy's memory. It also names my book, and hence, he found my email address.

"I want to express my deepest sympathy to you, losing such a beautiful soul as Marcy," he said. "I am deeply touched, saddened and feel so many other feelings that I can't even quite describe. I had heard many years ago that she died, but didn't really feel motivated to reach out for whatever reason, but here I am."

I remember this young man as being very sweet and kind to Marcy, and full of life and laughter. He spent time at our home and reminded me of a couple of times when he was invited to dinner and brought steaks for the barbeque that wouldn't even fit on a plate. He talked about how he and Marcy hiked up the mountain near the house, going up to Prescott and the cabin in the mountains we owned at the time, and the drive-in theaters where they never really watched the movie…So many memories for him.

I had mostly forgotten those times, but he still remembered everything. How much those times must have meant to him. It gave me an insight into his heart and how it, too, must have been broken when they split up and then when he heard she had died ten years later. "I got to reconnect with Marcy in 1991 just by a chance meeting in a local neighborhood hangout in Brentwood, west Los Angeles," he said. "It was really good to see her, and I couldn't believe how close we were living to each other at the time!"

"Marcy will always have a special place in my heart, and I think about her often," he said. "I am an emotional Pisces and for me, it is so hard to move on after such a tragedy."

Mostly, in his note, he spoke of what Marcy had meant to him and how very special she was, a confirmation of everything I feel also. Since this young man did not know any of Marcy's more recent friends, it is amazing how closely the feelings and reactions from him attune to what everyone said about her in other letters to me after her death. The phrases: amazing energy, had so much to give to the world, brought so much light unto others, we are all better for having known her…all so typical of how others saw her also. Now another person added to the list.

Most amazing was the fact that Marcy died on this young man's birthday, March 2, making it even harder for him to take.

"Thank you for bringing such a beautiful daughter into this world, who got to shine and bring so much light unto others," he added. "We are all better human beings having had Marcy in our lives for however long."

I do not know whether it was intentional or not, but after reading his letter, I still do not know much about him or what he did with his life after Marcy. He lives in Northern California right now. I would like to know, but maybe it was not meant to be. His letter only concentrated on Marcy, and then he offered me his deepest sympathy. I sent him a picture I have of Marcy and him from her photo album when they were 16-years-old, along with a copy of my first grief book. I hope he enjoys both, and perhaps I will hear from him again.

Thank you, young man, for a gift that came from your heart and now has touched mine forever.

Leaving a Legacy

One day in 2009, I went to an afternoon stage production with five friends. While waiting in line to get inside the theater, I saw an old acquaintance whose children knew my daughter Marcy. The mother and her son Mark were there to see the production also. Mark's wife wrote and starred in it.

After saying hello to the mother, she introduced me to her son. "Mark, this is Sandy Fox. Do you remember Sandy's daughter, Marcy Finerman?" Before Mark's mom could explain the circumstances now, Mark blurted out, "Yes," he said, his eyes lighting up, "we went to grade school together, and how is Marcy doing?"

I did not want to embarrass her son, but I had to say politely, "She was killed in a car accident 15 years ago."

Mark's mom was very embarrassed, but Mark did not miss a beat. "I'm so sorry," he said very sincerely. "Marcy and I were friends. I do remember her," he said. "Yes," I said to him, "I remember your name among her friends." I was looking at a 43-year-old man; the same age as Marcy would have been that particular year, but, of course, would have never recognized him. However, Mark's mom had remembered Marcy from almost 30 years ago, which I appreciated and saw as a precious gift.

Her gift was just mentioning Marcy's name. She didn't have to. She was aware of what had happened so long ago. Even though we had lost touch many years prior, she had heard the news and remembered it. Most bereaved parents want nothing more than for someone to acknowledge their child existed and is still remembered. Although I have nothing in common with Mark, the kindness on his face told me all I needed to know, and his mother's words allowed me to talk comfortably, even if briefly, about her and the situation. I explained how Marcy had graduated college and gotten a great job in

L.A., met the love of her life, Simon, and that she had been married only 4 ½ months before the accident.

We then parted as the play was about to start. One of my friends who was with me said, "It must feel good to have someone bring up your daughter's name and remember that they went to school together so long ago."

"Yes, very good," I said to my friend. To myself I thought, "You can't know how good!"

Knowing our children are remembered and live on in the hearts and lives of others is a measure of the wonderful legacy they have left us and everyone they knew and who knew them.

Old Friends Never Forget

I received an email from a good friend of my daughter from 30 years ago, who has tried to find me for many years. She had only my former married last name and did not know I had remarried. She was finally able to get my email. She had heard about Marcy's car accident years before and through her tears was writing to me.

"Some friendships," she said, "cannot be forgotten." I, too, was very friendly with her mother and somehow, as happens at times, we lost track of each other.

I called my daughter's friend immediately and we talked for a while. My daughter would have been 43 during 2009 when I heard from her, and it is hard to picture her friend as 42, married and worrying about her child serving in Iraq. She spoke of her mom and when we finished, I anxiously called her.

Time melted away, and it was as if we had just spoken the day before, not 20 years ago. It seems she, too, changed her name when she remarried, and that is why I could not find her. We are planning to have some fun times together. It is so hard to believe we have lived in the same city all these years and never bumped into each other. What we did discover was that we have mutual friends that we are both friendly with. We believe we will have a lot to talk about and catch up on when we meet, and hopefully, I will never lose track of her again as we grow old together.

I can't wait to bring my friend and her daughter the book I wrote about surviving grief, and show them precious pictures of Marcy, as we laugh at the antics of both Marcy and her daughter in their younger years. I am sure she will also share memories and some of her photos.

What happiness it brings to my heart to know that after all this time, Marcy's friends still bring me joy by staying in touch and remembering her. I was right all along. Her memory will live on.

8.　*Importance of Rituals*

Rituals are part of life. When your child dies, they become even more important. For myself, I have a few rituals I follow to honor and remember my daughter. Perhaps you will find or think of some rituals that will work for you.

Each time I travel for more than just a weekend, I first go to the cemetery to visit with Marcy and clean off her grave, placing new white silk flowers in the soft ground around the stone. I tell her where I am going and what I'll be doing on my trip, all the time wishing she could be going with me. I have noticed other stones in the cemetery look worn, old, and covered with mud. Obviously, relatives or even friends do not care for many of these stones. I am so tempted sometimes to go around and just wipe them, so that next to Marcy's they will look good, but the thought eventually passes. I have asked my husband and, as an alternative, Marcy's best friend, to take care of the stone after I am gone. It is important to me. Other occasions I definitely go to the cemetery are on her birthday and death date.

Her birthday is a simple affair, even though, at a younger age, she always had to have some type of party. In addition to going to the cemetery, we go out for dinner to a nice restaurant, toast her life and wish she were here with us. I know some of her friends have done the same thing and think of her on this day.

On Marcy's death date, I take out a few of her things and reminisce on her life, what she accomplished and what joy she brought to others and me in her 27 years.

On her wedding anniversary my ritual is to take out the video of her wedding (two hours plus) and watch it. Of course, she will never grow old or look old, but I do often wonder how she would look now as I watch it. I love seeing her personality and sense of humor shine though as she speaks on the video. Watching it always leaves me sad, and for days, I think of nothing else. It is something I must do to keep her close.

A close friend of hers also gave me a composite video of the last few years of her life that I watch. It is beautiful. Being a videographer he taped all the parties that both Marcy and others attended during the few years she was in Los Angeles. Then he spent the time going through each one and taking the sections dealing with Marcy and splicing them all together. I can see in this video how she loved life and all those who shared it with her. He then put music to the video interspersed with everyone saying a few words into the camera. It is 15 minutes long and easy to watch any time I feel like it. Those two videos are the only videos I have of her. When she was growing up, videos or DVD's was not part of our culture, unfortunately.

On all holidays during the year, I try to find a cause in which I can participate. For example, on Thanksgiving in past years I have fed the hungry at a soup kitchen, all the while thinking this is something Marcy might have done. On Christmas, I have donated needed items to the Veteran's Hospital in town and sent many cards to those who have no one else to celebrate with them. Everything I do is in honor and remembrance of my daughter.

My rituals are simple, yet satisfying. Each of you can do whatever helps you remember, with love, your special child.

9. *The Good That Can Come from Loss*

Is there anything good that comes from losing a child? At first all you feel is excruciating heartache, present loneliness, deep emptiness, the old life gone forever, the future a blur, the person you loved most in the world gone forever, and you…changed forever. Nothing is ever the same again. You are a different person. Days, months, years may pass and you cope as best you can.

Then out of the depth of grief and despair, grows something remarkable. You begin to see others in the same situation; some of them just moving on one day at a time, others deciding to do something with their lives as they now see that life…without their child. One bereaved parent meeting another, sharing stories, sharing memories, sharing hopes and dreams of a future they no longer have. Every one of them understands, for they have been there too. They understand as no one else can. There is a need that starts growing inside to do something in memory of the child, a need to show others there is hope and light at the end of a dark tunnel. Who better to do it? I, too, have been there.

"If I can help just one person, I have made a difference."

Since my daughter's death, I have met so many people I would have never met in my lifetime: good, kind, caring people who have lived through the worst possible thing that could ever happen to them, losing a child, two children, three children and up to five children

194

in a house fire. War, poverty and untold disasters...I have listened to many of these stories on television and read about others in the newspapers. Some I have even been fortunate to meet. What do many of these parents do? They turn right around and help the next one.

These and others I have met have done so much for others that it has encouraged me to go out and try to help others also. I find it so rewarding. My saying has become, "If I can help just one person, then I have made a difference." I do it always with my daughter in my mind and in my heart. I do it in her memory. I do it because I know that she, also, would have done what I do for others, even though, in a different situation. I know that because since she died, many tell me how she was the rock that bound everyone together. Such a wonderful thing to learn about your child, whom you knew deep down was good, but never realized how very good.

My life is so different than I would have ever imagined, and I wish I could share it with my daughter. I wish I could tell her about the diabetic mother whose life was saved by her daughter calling 911, only to have the daughter hit and killed by a drunk driver two months later, or the father whose child was abducted and murdered who went on to be a victim's rights advocate. I wish she knew about the book that came from deep inside me. No, it was not the great American novel, as Marcy would have wanted. It was simply about her and others who died unnecessarily. I began speaking to groups around the country about coping with grief. I have discovered in helping others, I also help myself. I continue to live my life to the fullest and best of my ability in all aspects, not only in dealing with the bereaved. I have activities like bridge and mah jongg that are relaxing and the many friends I have made have added enjoyment to my life. I feel comfortable talking about my daughter around all of them.

"In helping others, I also help myself."

I developed new goals. Some things that would have seemed a long time ago very important in my life no longer are significant. It is because I have already lost the one thing that always added meaning to my life. At one time, I dreamed of my life revolving around grandchildren and family. Now it is making a contented life with my new husband and enjoying as best I can what is left of the time I have here on earth.

I also look at things around me more closely now, a brilliant sunrise or sunset. I see beauty I never noticed before: the desert blooming, the baby birds nesting close by. It was always there. I was just too busy with the trivial things.

I am more sensitive to news stories on TV about children, about war, about the economy. I live more in the moment because I have discovered that sometimes 'tomorrow never comes."

Friends tell me they could not have survived losing a child. I look at each one and evaluate. Perhaps, some would never recover. However, most do recover, because they are survivors, just like me.

I believe that what I have done with my life is because of my daughter's life. The fact that she lived has made me a better person, the person I am today. Thank you, Marcy, for living, for changing the world in some small way and for continuing to help me make a difference. We can all make a difference in our own way, and I would encourage bereaved parents to have that goal.

10. Springtime Cleaning While Remembering

Another springtime cleaning is arriving. It is a time to clean house and yard, and, as I do so, just another season to think about how much I miss my daughter. She has been gone now for many years. As I clean the house, I glance at the boxes in my closet of what is left of her life. It is compacted into a small corner of the closet and after dusting them, I open the boxes.

Not that much is there. They include speech debate awards and trophies, writings she did when she was only 5-years-old and writings during her time as marketing director of the Music Center in Los Angeles. Childhood items and scrapbook items from plays she saw and parties she attended, the Girl Scout badges she earned, all the notes and remembrances from others after her death, and, most of all, the photos are also there. Photos from birth to death that are worth a thousand words, a lifetime of memories that Marcy took and kept in albums of family and friends.

...a photo of Charlton Heston with his arm around Marcy... when he performed at the Music Center.

I look at the albums occasionally and reminisce: a photo of Charlton Heston with his arm around Marcy is there, when he performed at the Music Center. Marcy had to spend a lot of time with him to help do the publicity and got to know him. "What a kind man," she told me. "He is by far the nicest movie star I've met." She always spoke of the stars who were exasperating to work around, the singers who would give special performances on the plaza, and the musicians who she got to hear play beautiful music like Yo-Yo Ma.

I have given away many things, some to her friends who asked for a piece of jewelry, a dress, or an object she may have purchased on a trip. A piece of jewelry is not a problem; she had quite a lot, and I'm happy to have her friends enjoy earrings or a necklace (I have many to enjoy also); a dress, yes, that's okay as long as it doesn't fit me (some of her things did, and I still wear them). The art objects I don't give away. Those are mine alone, and I won't part with them. They include a beautiful Venetian glass decanter and matching glasses as well as Russian dolls, glass fishes and English Wedgwood objects bought on Marcy's travels. I retrieved these items from her condominium after the accident. I have merged them with all of my own travel collection, since she and I both loved traveling and seeing the world. I do admire her excellent taste in choosing not the most expensive but simple elegant items.

As I move from one room to the next dusting and cleaning, I see the photos I have placed all over the house among other photos of family and friends. There is at least one photo of Marcy in every room. Some may think that morbid, but I find it comforting to walk from one room to the next and see her smiling face. Among them are her engagement picture; her wedding picture; a photo of Marcy and her best friend Lynn; one of Marcy, her father; and me and one of her in Disneyland hugging Pluto, the dog. I have one showing three generations: my mom, Marcy and myself at age 13 and then the three of us again on a vacation in St. Thomas 10 years later. I remember we laughed most of the trip because my mom's luggage never arrived, and we had to shop for all new clothes. Marcy had a great time because, as she told me secretly, "Now we can get Grandma some stylish clothes to wear!"

Best of all, I have a series of 16 photos from birth through age 16 (most are from her yearly school pictures) hanging on the wall and showing the transformation of what she looked like from birth to her teen years. I wipe them all down as I dust and lovingly hold them all as I think of those times so long ago. I would never put these photos in a closet.

I also have all her stuffed animals she loved. There must be about 50 of them, some large, some small. First, I thought I'd give them away to the children's hospital, since I am not fortunate to have grandchildren, but I've found it hard to let go of them, so

---

I have about 50 stuffed animals...I've found it hard to let go of them...

I keep them all in a special guest room of the house, wiping them off, looking at them and remembering where they all came from. Pluto was one of her favorites, picked out at Disneyland when she was 10-years-old. Another, a huge bear about three feet high that she won at a carnival sits on the floor (too big to put on a shelf). A Hawaiian bear is there as are many examples of Garfield. Beanie bears and a Scottish bear are also among the lot. Since I have Godchildren, I occasionally give one to them on a special occasion if they ask to have it. One day I hope I will be able to part with at least half of them, but the rest will always stay with me because of the good memories they bring back.

As I finish the springtime cleaning of dusting, vacuuming and washing everything in sight for one more year, I'm glad that I had the opportunity to remember with love many of the good times for all of us. We never forget, no matter how long it is. There is healing in remembering, and I choose to leave these footprints in my heart forever.

11. Kennedy Assassination Becomes Personal

Just as we all remember where we were and what we were doing on Sept. 11, 2001, those of us who were around Nov. 22, 1963, also remember exactly what we were doing and where we were when President John F. Kennedy was shot and killed.

I had been married four months, attending college that day, and went up to my sorority in the dorm on campus for lunch. Everyone appeared to be glued to the television, and I asked why. The news on television told us that Kennedy was shot in a Dallas motorcade and the world was waiting for news of his condition. Then the announcement by newscaster Walter Cronkite as he took of his glasses and solemnly told us the president was dead. The shock, the tears, the uncertainty of what would happen echoed around the world for a much beloved person. It was not the first assassination of a president, or the last attempt on future ones.

Camelot is what they used to call the Kennedy reign. We all reveled in it, wishing our lives were as perfect as theirs seemed for a time. Their Camelot turned out to be devastating as one of the Kennedy's children died a few days after birth from illness, John was assassinated, Jacque died from cancer, and finally, John Jr. died in a plane crash with his fiancé, Carolyn Bessette and Carolyn's sister. John Jr's sister, Caroline, is the only surviving member of that side of the Kennedy family.

My mind then switches to the day my daughter died, a different kind of shock, rivers of tears, the uncontrollable grief, and the unbelievable reality that it had become personal for me. It is a day I will never forget either, March 2, 1994. I moved around in

---

John F. Kennedy died Nov. 22, 1963.
Marcy Lewis died March 2, 1994.
They share an unfulfilled destiny.

---

numbness because, of course, the accident did not seem real. Nothing would happen to my beautiful daughter, I thought. She was safe in the loving arms of her husband. For many months, I was sure my daughter would knock on the door and surprise me with a visit as she had done many times before. It was a long time before I truly realized that I would never see her again.

This is true for many bereaved parents. It is inconceivable to most of us who have lost a child that the child is gone. We keep things as they are for quite a long time or sometimes forever: the clothes, jewelry, toys, stuffed animals, awards and any items identifying our child. We hope someone will tell us it was all a cruel joke. When reality eventually sets in, it is almost like a second period of mourning. We start comparing the death with others.

It is then I realize I can also focus on all the good moments with my daughter: a first birthday party, her first steps, her first school day, her first award in school for writing or being on the debate team, her first car at 16, a special vacation we took together, her wedding day, all these things and more. Then my heart bursts with love, pleasure, and happiness that I was able to share all these things with her. I know I will never forget them. I try to share them with others who care.

I will always remember the day my daughter died, just as I will always remember when President Kennedy died. Two lives, destined not to have their dreams fulfilled - something Marcy and the President will always share.

12. If My Child Had Lived, What Would Life Be Like?

What would my life have been like if my daughter were alive today? I often think of that question and ponder the answers, as I'm sure most bereaved parents do. It is part of the grieving process.

I envision all sorts of scenarios filled with friends, family and famous people. Marcy and her husband would be giving many parties. They were both involved in the Hollywood scene as producer and marketing director and were meeting many new people in 1994 when she died. Back in 1992, Marcy knew how much I liked Barry Manilow, so when she found out that as part of her job, she was in charge of a reception at which he was singing, she invited me to come to Los Angeles, pretend I was one of the hosts and enjoy the performance up close and personal. The one condition was that I had to wear a black long skirt and a white fancy blouse as all the hosts would be dressed that way. "That is no problem," I told her. I was thrilled and did attend, greeted many stars and superstars and listened to Barry Manilow sing many songs before he hurried out the back door. I had a great time and think of how many occasions like that there would have been in both our futures.

I often wonder if Marcy would have stayed in that position or tried for a more important job. Her major in college was advertising and her creative mind would have worked well in this field. I can visualize her starting a new advertising agency and from all the contacts she had made in her previous job, get many clients for her new business. I would be so proud watching the business grow and knowing she was so successful.

After Marcy married, I went to Los Angeles for visits and there was talk of buying a new home. I was so excited to tour some of the homes with her to see what was available. For what they could afford at the time, there was not much that was either bigger than two bedrooms or that did not need a lot of work. I thought that after retiring from teaching a few years later, there would be plenty of time to go back and forth. I would have loved helping her decorate a new home, visit with them and talk of the future. When I decorate or redecorate my home now, I think of how Marcy and I had the same taste and how much she would have liked to help me also.

I envision a scenario with grandchildren. Marcy loved children and always told me she wanted many. Although I remember telling her I would not be able to run to Los Angeles every time she needed a babysitter, I knew that if something important came up, I would not be able to say no. I can imagine a couple of girls and one boy. After her death her best friend had two boys and a girl (the girl was named Marcy) and I am now the Godparent for them. I am thrilled to have that role, but, of course, still yearn for what will never be.

Marcy was a very friendly person that enjoyed people. It would not surprise me if, in the future, she would have won awards for all the organizations she belonged to and all the philanthropic projects she was involved in. I can visualize traveling to L.A. many times to be present at those ceremonies that would honor her and play my part, the proud mother.

I am a traveler, and Marcy had the travel bug. I could see all of us traveling together, particularly on cruises, throughout the world. Now I travel with my husband and think of how much Marcy would love some of these places I visit. When I travel, I wear a necklace with her picture on it so that she is always with me. One incident always stands out in my mind back in the eighties in Europe. I am still amazed at the outcome of our separate trips we planned. How we were going to meet on a specific day and time in Interlaken, Switzerland. "Let's make a pact," I told Marcy. "Wherever you will be coming from with your friend, get into Interlaken on the 6 p.m. train, and I will meet you at the station." We didn't talk for three weeks before that day because her itinerary was very up in the air. My husband was skeptical at the loose arrangements we made, but when she stepped off that train at

6 p.m. and waved to me, I marveled at how we had accomplished meeting halfway around the world with very little communication in-between. This summer when we arrived by train in Interlaken, I stepped off the train and happy memories came flooding back.

Marcy had many goals for herself that she was not able to accomplish because of her sudden death. I cannot even begin to imagine all that she would have done and how proud I would have continued to be of her. Not a moment goes by that I do not think of her and how in a split second, one's life can change forever. However, I cling to the happy memories I do have, as all parents must, and understand that has to be enough.

13. A Trip to the Cemetery

I don't mind going to the cemetery. It is where my daughter is and always will be. I make a special effort to go on her death day, her birthday, sometimes near my birthday, her wedding anniversary and any time before I leave on a long trip. My average is about four to five times a year.

I drive to the center of the tree lined pathway, park the car, take cleaning tools, flowers, a large blanket to sit on and then walk to the area where her stone is. I place the new white silk lilies (her favorite) next to the stone (they last for months) and replace the old ones. I never bring fresh flowers, only silk ones. Fresh ones never last long; silk ones do.

I look at the picture of her that I had embossed on the marble and see a bright, happy, smiling Marcy as she was many years ago for her engagement picture, full of life, full of hopes and dreams for her future. I scrape the section of the marble that has the picture embedded in it until the residue is gone. Then I clean off the actual marble stone, which has developed a lot of calcium built up from both rain and watering of the lawn. I like to have it clean for anyone who might visit. When I am done, it is usually the shiniest stone there.

As I look around at other graves, no one else seems to do what I will keep on doing for as long as I live. I am a Virgo and Virgos are perfectionists, very neat, organized people. I attribute many of my actions to my astrological sign.

I bought the plot next to Marcy to assure we will always be close. Marcy's Dad also bought one near her. It is a good feeling to have that done and not have to think about it.

I no longer ask why this happened to Marcy, to me, to everyone who loved her. I know there is no answer and you end up just accepting this as the way it is. This doesn't mean I don't get sad or angry at the way life has turned out for all of us. I still have my moments but as time goes on, I am calmer and more practical.

I like talking to Marcy and telling her my latest adventures and the latest gossip, which I know she would love to hear. I sometimes chuckle and can almost hear her laughing with me. Oh, we did have such great times together and many memories are inside my head.

One day a relative called me to tell me of an unusual experience he had at the cemetery in March 2006. His parents are buried there also, so when he goes, he also stops at Marcy's stone, which is close by. I was having a very serious surgery that day and when he went to Marcy's stone, he said something strange happened. For a split second, he could see a halo around Marcy's picture and her saying to him, "Don't worry, Mom will be all right." He was afraid to tell me of this experience because he thought I might think him crazy, but I certainly don't. I know things like that have happened to others, and I just smiled when I heard his story. The surgery, by the way, was a success.

I find it interesting that a cemetery is a place of peace, quiet and solitude that people can go to be with a loved one for just a while; yet, how many take advantage of that? I realize some may have their reasons for not going there, and a number of people find it morbid. I am not one of those, and I will continue to observe special days and certain anniversaries and find comfort in being close to my daughter.

14. Passing a Grief Milestone

One Saturday in 2009 was a milestone for me. For the first time in almost 15 years, I was able to do something I thought I would never be able to do again, drive a car with a child in the back seat.

When Marcy died and Lynn, her best friend, had children (naming her daughter Marcy after my Marcy), I was thrilled to become their official Godmother. As her three children grew, I became involved in their lives, seeing them for birthdays, many holidays and on sleepovers at my home. Only one problem existed. If we were to go out somewhere, either Lynn or my husband Lawrence had to drive. I could not drive and have the kids in the car. As long as someone else drove, I was comfortable about being in the car with one or all of them.

An impaired driver killed my Marcy, and in my mind, I could not take the responsibility of having my Godchildren's lives in my hands and wonder if another impaired driver could possibly cause an accident hurting my Godchildren in any way. I realize this may have been over-reacting on my part, but that is how I felt, and I had to follow those feelings.

For all these years, that is how we have operated. Lynn would bring the kids over to play or sleepover, but we never went anywhere that involved a car unless someone else could drive. That Saturday Lynn, the kids and I were going to the movies. Both Lynn and I had to drive to the theater separately because I had to be somewhere else right afterwards. I anticipated little Marcy wanting to drive with me, and I was right. I made a decision that it was time to face that demon. Marcy, of course, knew nothing of my fear, and we chatted as we drove to the theater.

Was I scared? I was petrified, nervous and, of course, very careful on a before Christmas crowded freeway with thousands going shopping. I drove slowly; I kept to the right; I looked in the mirror constantly and kept a watchful eye for any erratic drivers on the road. We chatted. She asked about my Marcy, wanted to know more about the person for whom she was named and even asked me how she died. I told her, deciding she was old enough to know the whole story.

In the process of talking and watching the road, time passed, and I arrived at the theater, met Lynn and her son Jonah a few minutes later and felt good about what I had accomplished. I breathed a sigh of relief and said to myself, "You did it." Some of us have situations like this that we must face and when we do, it is a relief to know that we have accomplished what we consider a milestone. Now, I am on to the next goal for myself.

I do not know when I will be able to take all three children in my car, but as they say, one step at a time… as it was when my Marcy died…one step at a time towards recovery.

15. Working on Recovering From a Child's Death

I am continually working on recovering from the death of my daughter. What do I do?

Foremost, I think of the wonderful times we had together talking, going shopping, traveling, and going to theater shows. She would ask my opinion on most topics that were on her mind and even followed my suggestions on some of them. Even if she did her own thing, I was happy to know she thought enough of my opinion to ask.

I talk about my daughter whenever possible to whoever will listen. I test people. Will they ignore my comments or will they pick up the conversation and continue to talk about an event of which my daughter was a part? Good friends feel more comfortable doing that. I believe you can eventually make everyone comfortable and let him or her know you want your child to always be a part of the conversation. The real joy comes when, on their own, a question is asked about her (Didn't she win some trophies at a speech tournament in high school?), and I can respond with joy in my heart. Best of all, they will listen with interest to what I have to say and suddenly she is alive in all our hearts for just a few minutes.

Crying is triggered at very unusual times. I could just be driving from one area to another and it will hit me. "She is gone. I can't talk to her. I can't call her and tell her what happened to me today." It can be a song, an anniversary, a beautiful sunset that can set me off, but fortunately, it doesn't last long. I don't let the memories consume me, but strangely enough, I feel better after a little cry.

I help other bereaved parents when I can. I speak at national conferences about coping, have held two national bereavement conferences in my hometown, and on a local level, I helped start and am a part of a bereavement group for parents who have lost their only child or all their children. I try to give back when I can, and it has been so rewarding to meet the parents who you feel a great affinity to. Only those who have gone through it know the feelings involved.

I continue to write. My first book is still selling, and now another one. I hope that my blog I write once a week on Sunday is of help to others on their grief journey. I freelance articles to magazines, and I write for the Open to Hope Foundation that is reaching millions every year.

I continue to travel, always keeping my daughter in my heart every place I go. I tell my husband, who now travels with me, when we are in areas that Marcy and I went to long ago. If I go to a new location, I think of how Marcy may like the location and what her comments would be. She is always with me on my travels and in my heart.

The last time I saw my daughter was at the airport. She was leaving to go home to California after her best friend's wedding. Ironically, she had to attend a funeral in California, and she came towards me smiling giving me a big long hug. I held her tight for a few seconds, almost as though I sensed the future. I couldn't remember the last time I had held her like that, but my mind lingered on how wonderful she felt in my arms, a grown up child who had just married herself months before and was ecstatically happy. With her sudden death a week later, there was never a chance to say good-bye, but I did tell her I loved her as she walked into the airport terminal.

Dealing with the death of my daughter is the greatest challenge I face and will continue to face for the rest of my life.

16. A Moment in Time Has Profound Affect on Personal Journey

We remember moments in our lives that have profound effects on us…and there is probably not a person in America that cannot tell you where they were on Sept. 11, 2001, the day our world changed forever. Not only can I tell you where I was, but how in my own way, my involvement in that day will stay with me always.

My first grief book had been out for about five months at the time, and I was doing some book tours around the U.S. I enjoyed speaking to groups at bookstores and to bereavement groups on surviving grief in addition to meeting all the parents I was eventually to see again many years later when speaking at national bereavement conferences. This specific book tour took me to New Jersey bookstores and support groups in the area. I was to be there 3-4 days. As it turned out, I was there 10 days before I could get a plane to return home. I met many people who had lost loved ones or friends at the World Trade Center while I was doing my book tour.

Because of a mechanical problem with the aircraft I was on into Newark, instead of landing at 9 p.m. on September 10, 2001, I landed on September 11 at 3 a.m. and went directly to the Days Inn at the airport for the night. The next morning I was to appear on a daily TV news show and talk about my book. That did not happen for another six months, when I returned to New Jersey for another tour with my book.

I woke up to the total destruction of the World Trade Center and for days from across the river, could see the smoke-filled air miles wide, causing coughing and breathing problems for many. My book signings went on as scheduled, with a few people showing up at each, not what I had hoped to see. Most were glued to their TV sets or mourning those who lost their lives. I kept thinking about how my book could be any timelier then at this moment. I had just written about surviving grief and the families of these thousands of people were just starting their grief journey. If I could help just one person with my book, it would be comforting to me personally.

Of those who did come to the book signings or bereavement group meetings, one woman had a friend whose son had still not been heard from five days later. The mother still hoped. Another had just spoken to her cousin who had her son pulled out of the building alive. Still another lost her husband when his fire unit went into the building to help survivors. Many from his unit had also perished. Those who wanted to donate blood could not. Hospitals had run out of blood bags. Internet and phone service was down, so many did not and could not hear from loved ones those first few days. Picture ID's and proof of residency were needed in areas close to the disaster. A bomb threat to the Empire State Building caused evacuation of all buildings in the area. Cameras captured actions on the ground and words in the air. Burned into memory are shouts and mumbled prayers.

There were also pockets of order where command posts with volunteers handed out bottled water and food. Police, firefighters, bureaucrats, contractors, military, doctors, nurses, clergy and even thieves gathered to give what help they could.

The horrendous idea that thousands of people fell to their death in the hole made by 110 floors worth of rubble and medal was unthinkable. Most of those people were dead; a few lucky ones saved.

Being at a bereavement group meeting and talking about grieving and coping with a loss as I wrote about in my book was comforting for many people. There were so many stories, so many people, and so much sadness, and here they could express heartbreaks, fears and hopes.

Even though my daughter had been dead for seven years by then, I knew what these people were feeling. I understood their tears, their silent screams, and their overwhelming sense of loss. It would be a long time before they could get on with their lives.

That week was a moment in time that to this day, I still remember and think about as the start of my own personal journey with my book that opened up a whole new world to me, a world of speaking and helping bereaved parents in any way I could.

17. Corresponding With Bereaved Parents

One morning I opened my email and heard from a mother who had lost her 21-month-old son in a car/pedestrian accident last year. She had just finished reading my book, *I Have No Intention of Saying Good-bye*, saying it was the first one she had read since the accident, and found that reading about other parents who have lost children and what they have gone through reaffirms her own feelings. She, like many, is having a rough time.

In another email I received recently a mother said she read my book twice, enjoying it more the second time and got even more out of it. She appreciated how well I expressed what she has been and is still feeling.

Still another person said, "After reading your book, I feel less alone in this mess."

I could go on and on about the hundreds of letters I've received over the years. The important thing here is to emphasize to all reading this that corresponding with bereaved parents is a good outlet to express your feelings and for the person to whom you are writing, to share a part of himself/herself with you. By sharing, you begin to realize that whatever you are feeling is probably very normal and that all of us must go through these feelings to get to the other side. What is on the other side? I call it hope. We do eventually get better, although we never forget. Time is a great healer.

I encourage you to do whatever is necessary to find a few parents in your situation and begin corresponding with them. Keep a copy of all correspondence and later on look back to see how much you have grown. You will see there will be growth, and there will be new beginnings you may never have dreamed could happen. Bereaved parents who have gone into the valley and out again may have suggestions for a particular cause for you to get involved with, one that perhaps your child may have been interested in. They could suggest different volunteer organizations that might be of interest. Listen to them and try some of their suggestions. There is a life on the other side that you can be a part of and enjoy.

Where can you find these bereaved parents? Contact any bereavement organization such as Compassionate Friends or Alive Alone (if you had an only child or all your children have died). If your child died of SIDS, AIDS or any other specific illness, those support groups can also help. Tell them what you are looking for, and they will either give you the information you seek or make sure someone you can talk to contacts you. I believe your best bet is a local chapter of these groups. The national organizations can give you local information. Contact the leader, tell your situation and go from there.

One mother sent me a thank you card after I spoke at her Compassionate Friends chapter. The note was very nice, but the quote on the front has stuck with me. "You can't change the direction of the wind, but you can adjust your sails." We cannot bring our children back, much as we would like to, but we can still find a different type of joy in our lives and grow from there.

18. Grief Triggers

No matter how long ago our child died, we all have grief triggers. There are moments when, unexpectedly, someone says or does something to bring our focus back to our child who we have so carefully placed in a corner of our heart. In those moments, we remember everything, and our reaction may be to smile and simply go on as though nothing has happened or we may get an excruciating pain in our chest that may make it difficult to breathe and/or talk normally.

I am more of the latter. My heart will beat fast, and I may have to take deep breaths. I imagine that everyone can hear my heart pounding as the memories wash over me. I make a concerted effort, without saying a word, to continue with what I was doing at the time and to slow the heart rate. The memories linger, sometimes pleasantly, sometimes too long, and I am caught in a conundrum of remembering feelings, days, months, years, that I love to think about, but know that those memories are no longer part of my reality.

The anniversaries of my daughter's death, March 2, and her birthday, July 27, are not good days for me. I try to keep busy, and I honor those days by reflecting on her life, looking at pictures and watching the only two videos I have of her. I remember what one of her dear friends said to me after her death. "She touched all of us in a way that can never be forgotten." Her friend felt a quote by May Sarton said it all. I quote: *She became for me an island of light, fun and wisdom where I could run with my discoveries, torments and hopes at any time of the day and find welcome.* Yes, a very appropriate quote to describe Marcy.

Holidays, where families get together such as Thanksgiving or Mother's Day, are particularly hard. Those two holidays it seems, are for families to be together, whether it is to give thanks or to honor Mothers. I feel very lost on Mother's Day since I am the only one of my family left. There is only my husband to wish me a happy day, and I am so thankful he is there to help me get through these days.

Sometimes I will hear songs that Marcy used to like or a song that reminds me of a part in a school play she had, and I can hear her singing it loudly and clearly. (Her voice was always much better than mine; I have trouble carrying a tune!). I smile when I think of the two of us singing songs together and dancing in the living room. They are good memories.

When I am traveling and going to places I know she has been with a friend or me, I become sad, knowing she loved traveling as much as I do. At times, I am not only sad but also mad that she will never be able to enjoy new places, new experiences, and new friends. I travel now not only for my own enjoyment but also for Marcy's. I go places I think she would enjoy and smile to myself as I see her climbing the hill imitating Julie Andrews singing, and I wear my Marcy picture necklace whenever I travel so that I feel she is always with me.

These triggers and others I deal with as best as I can. I try to be good to myself and to others. I treasure my good friends and my wonderful husband. Know that whether it's one, two, five, ten or twenty years, you will never forget. Try to work through the grief triggers that will always come when you least expect them to, and make them a positive experience by thinking of some good times that came from them.

19. Sharing Memories Helps Grieving Families

Sharing memories after the death of a child can help the grieving family more than you will ever know.

If you were close to the child who died, there are many things you can do to help, but the absolute best is to help keep their memory alive by sharing precious moments you had with the child, whether it was a school function, a working environment, a party or just a fun evening at one of the homes. Here are some examples of my own experience when my daughter died.

Even those who did not know my daughter Marcy were able to share something comforting. I met the couple who happened to be right behind her car accident. I did not know any circumstances of the accident and was eager to hear what they had to say. They were able to give me a minute-by-minute description of what they had seen. You see, they knew my daughter's husband through work, but had never met Marcy. They did not recognize either of them because the new car, which they had just driven off the dealer's lot, was unrecognizable and Marcy's husband was pinned underneath parts of the debris. They politely asked me if I wanted to know the details as they saw the accident unfold.

I said, "Yes, I want to know everything you can tell me. No one else could do that." Therefore, they did. They particularly spoke of how a paramedic was two cars away and tried for 20 minutes to resuscitate Marcy. They took Simon the few blocks to the hospital, knowing he had life-threatening injuries. They stayed and watched the time unfold and the obviously distraught expression and mannerisms of the paramedic, knowing after a few minutes there was nothing he could do to help Marcy. It was important to hear from them that she looked peaceful, as though she was just asleep. It was also comforting to know she did not suffer. It was an instant death. This couple took the time to tell it like it happened. I appreciated their honesty and will always cherish knowing the facts from an eyewitness.

Marcy's boss at work told an interesting story about why he hired Marcy for the marketing director job at the L.A. Music Center. "I remember Marcy arriving early for that first interview. She told me she had scoped out the area in downtown L.A. to make sure she knew where the building was, how to get there and where to park. Being late was not in her character and she made sure she had all the answers she needed to get there and get the job. I was so impressed with her answers to all my questions that I hired her on the spot. The other candidate came in late because she had not "done her homework" as Marcy had to find the interview spot and parking area. In my office was someone who knew about people and life, someone to bounce ideas off, someone you could go to for advice on any problem. Personal or business, she always had the best answers."

Another story told by Marcy's pre-school teacher and good friend of the family who said, "Marcy wore a new poncho that her grandmother knitted for her. I told her it was lovely. 'Do you think, I asked her, that I could borrow it sometime?' (I am a very small woman...4 feet, 8 inches.) Marcy eyed me up and down and then said, 'Mrs. Richman, not now. You can borrow it when I grow up!' What a gal!"

A friend of Marcy's dad said that he knew Marcy as a baby and his most vivid memory was the first time he met her. "I will always think of her as the spaghetti face kid. One day I walked into your home and there she was, sitting in her high chair, covered with spaghetti. Even then, she was the organizer and the arranger. She had reorganized and rearranged not only her upper torso, the high chair, and the floor but also the whole kitchen had become the spaghetti kitchen. She was so proud of what she had done. Her little face displayed pride and humor. Even at that tender young age, she knew what she was doing. She did it well, she did it with humor and she did it with excellence, perfection and character."

A co-worker of Marcy has said simply, "I like to think that Marcy's supreme logic will continue to guide me through my job and that she is now in a wonderful place…probably finding a fourth for tennis."

Another of her friends had a cute story: "When I was admiring her beautiful engagement ring from Simon, Marcy said, "I just made him take me to Tiffany's first, and then every place else seemed so reasonable!"

The mother of one of her best friends recalls that on the day of the Northridge earthquake, Jan. 17, 1994 (two weeks before her death) Marcy called her in Tucson because she thought the mom might be worried about my daughter, Lori. She wanted to ease her mind. Lori was out of town and she should not worry about her when she tried to call and couldn't reach her. "I thought that was so sweet of her to think of me at a time like that, when she was under the kitchen table!" said the mom.

As time passed I received over 100 notes and stories from Marcy's friends, about what a good friend she was and how she held groups of people together with her friendship and kindness. It was comforting to know how much she was loved and that she left a legacy for others to emulate. I have kept all the letters and notes and occasionally like to read them.

At her funeral, more than 300 people attended. Some gave eulogies and spoke of what she meant to them. It does help in the grief process to know that so many admired your child. I was told a year later near the anniversary of the accident that some of her friends got together at a restaurant to talk and reminisce about her. One of her friends was kind enough to call and tell me about the meeting. There were funny stories and thoughtful moments. All their comments were precious memories to keep within my heart.

The testimonies of people regarding those who die are witness to what kind of young people they were. I would encourage anyone has the opportunity and ability to share something comforting with the remaining family after the death of a child to do just that.

20. Redefining Our Lives After a Child's Death

My daughter, who died in a car accident almost five months after her marriage, never lived to see her first wedding anniversary. Her dreams and hopes for the future are gone. My hopes for her: a family, a bright future, a wonderful marriage, they are all gone.

Each year I think what her life would have been like now. She would have had children to love and share with her husband; she probably would have had a career in the advertising or public relations field. On the other hand, perhaps she would have preferred staying home and just be a mother. They would have traveled eventually, seen the world, learned from the experiences and been better people for it. Perhaps my grandchildren would have done something special in this world and for this world. I dream of all that and then I see how what has happened has changed me forever. In some ways, it has made me a better person.

"You are a very special person," a friend says to me. "You made the best of what has happened to you. I couldn't have done it." (Of course, you could have, I think to myself.)

"I don't know how you lived through it," says one mother to me. "What choice did I have at the time," I say to her. "You just do."

"Does time really heal your wounds, your heart?" asks another mother. "Do you ever get over it? "No," I answer. "You never fully heal; you never get over it; you never forget."

However, we do change. As time moves forward, we can all move forward. We can do what is best for us. It may not be what we originally thought we would do, but it can still be meaningful.

People have come into my life and become part of it in ways I never imagined. I thought I would always teach; I retired three years after my daughter died, but in a way, I am still teaching, teaching others how to survive a child's death, teaching others about the grief journey. Strangely enough, as much as it may help them, it still helps me too. I continue to learn from others. I continue to grow. It is a sign I am recovering…slowly and continually.

We redefine ourselves with the choices we make. We actually choose how we will survive. We can decide whether we are going to be bitter, or we can open ourselves to changes, confront the lessons of grief and treat them as opportunities for growth. Because of what has happened to us, we can learn to have greater courage. We can learn to appreciate different aspects of life that we took for granted before. We can learn the importance of reaching out to others in the same situation, which may not be at the same destination but are on the same journey, and we can learn a deeper compassion for others. These are but a few of the lessons of grief that can lead us to a new joy for living if we allow them to.

I think friend Bob Baugher, bereaved parent and psychology instructor at Highline Community, said it best: *My precious child…I am because of you. Your child is your child because of you. You are the person you are today because of your child; not because of your child's death, but because of your child's life. He lived. She lived. You live… and who would you have been without this wonderful human being, who came into your life and changed it forever.*

Those who have lost a child ask me, "What magical thing will happen to me that will make me feel better? It's been so long." Don't be impatient. There is no magic. The fact that you want to feel better and move on with your life after the loss of a child is a good sign. What you do not realize is that it may take a very long time. Each of us reacts differently. Each of us heals differently. There is no set time that you should be well and functioning again. Your mind and body will do a lot of the work for you. You may be able to do it yourself, you may have family and friends to help you or you may need professional help. You are in a very vulnerable period of your life; healing is questionable. Do what is best for you using the resources available to you.

Only time and meeting others in your same situation will make you feel better. Talk to them. Listen to them. Find out what they have done, how they have coped and, in turn, it will help you cope.

Part 5

Ten Inspirational Stories From Bereaved Parents

Each one of these personal stories reflects both the single parent and couple's thoughts of how they are moving on and living their lives without their child. Stressed in these uplifting stories are learning recovery techniques, rediscovering who we are and finding out how we can help others. Take the love you shared with your child into a future filled with promise and hope. Let these parents guide you and give you ideas to be able to move forward with your life.

When you are sorrowful look again in your heart,
and you shall see that in truth you are weeping
for that which has been your delight.

- Kahlil Gibran

1. A Parent's Worst Nightmare: Jeanne's Story

"Danny died of a football size fast-growing tumor in his abdomen...within 24 hours of his diagnosis, he was gone...He had Burkitts Lymphoma, a disease with less than a 10 percent chance of survival."

When Jeanne and Ray's son, Danny, died, Jeanne says it was like a road falling away from her. "I was numb. I didn't even know what I was doing or know how I would survive one hour, one day. We were so devastated, unable to comprehend how we, as parents, couldn't save our child. We asked, 'Why did we deserve this? Why us?'"

This is a common feeling of most bereaved parents. Jeanne was to find out it was just the beginning of what will be a lifetime journey for her, filled with many highs and lows.

Ten days after Danny's death at age 3½, Jeanne attended a Compassionate Friends meeting where she found comfort and companionship from those who understood what she was going through. "The group gave me the support I needed to keep going," she said. "I knew I had to be there for my other sons."

Danny, born Jan. 20, 1993, died of a football size fast-growing tumor in his abdomen. The doctors did exploratory surgery, but Danny did not survive. Within 24 hours of his diagnosis, he was gone. He had Burkitts Lymphoma, a disease with less than a 10 percent chance of survival.

In addition to grieving for Danny, Jeanne later noticed one of her other sons, Adam, was entirely quiet. He did no babbling or talking and at 2-years-old was diagnosed with apraxia, a severe neurological speech disorder that controls the input from the brain to the oral motor muscles providing speech. "It is like having a loose wire or connection in the brain. It is a frustrating disorder for both parents and the child to deal with."

"What happens is that children cannot produce the correct sounds to verbally make themselves understood and the words come out garbled," she explained. "It is very difficult to detect in a child's early years of development. Because the child cannot phonetically break down words, there are many learning issues? It is hard for them to read and they have trouble processing."

Intelligence leveling in most children with apraxia is unaffected. For example, Adam could put together 60-piece puzzles without ever having seen them before. Emotionally it is hard for him to know how to say what he wants, and he can become very frustrated. He was also socially deficient and didn't know proper etiquette because he didn't have the ability to learn when growing up at first. Little by little, as he grew, his condition improved. Intensive speech therapy was the key in helping him once diagnosed. He used a special computer device to help him communicate and slowly started communicating. He is now doing well in special schools, with some mainstream classes.

Because Jeanne knew nothing at the time about this condition and could not find any help, she ended up starting her own non-profit to disseminate information, articles and support. "There were four meetings a year with fabulous speakers coming to each one," she said. Lack of support from people has caused her this year to stop the meetings. People still email her, though, and she tries to help each one. The non-profit will continue, but without meetings for now.

"As a parent, I cannot stress how important it is to educate medical professionals, teachers and parents about apraxia," she said. "When Adam was diagnosed, I didn't know where to turn for help. If more professionals knew about this disorder, many more parents of diagnosed or undiagnosed children would know there is hope and information that can help them. It is important to catch the disorder early on."

Her third son, Josh, is autistic. "It was hard to get his attention. He wouldn't answer to his name; he was in his own world," she said. "He would eventually 'script', in other words, he would use phrases he saw on television." Now we are talking about a whole different kind of therapy."

In addition to day-by-day dealing with the death of one child, she had two special needs children to raise. Throughout all this, her husband, Ray, was very supportive. He retired in 2006 because he wanted to be with the kids and help her in the day-to-day routine. "He took the kids on trips and was a great father. He also had additional problems to deal with personally. He internalized a lot and didn't talk much about what was bothering him." In early 2010, Ray died suddenly. The support she had treasured is no longer there with her husband gone.

"It is really tough on me now, Jeanne said. "My mountain is gone. It was hard enough when Danny died, but I still had Ray. Now I have no one."

For a long time Jeanne wrote poetry and found that it helped her considerably to deal with her life, then and now. She went to grief therapy for a while after Danny died but found that the therapist (who had never lost a child) did not get it. She also went to see a therapist after her husband died.

At a friend's suggestion, what she has found that helps her now, is scheduling people for dinner every week at her house. She has friends, family members and Ray's friends from work come over. "Having people over who care and also hurt because of my losses is a good feeling. I hope to continue this tradition for a long time."

Jeanne realizes it will be a tough road, but knows she can make it through. The comfort and help that she gets is extremely beneficial to her and encourages her to help others in the same situation.

Danny died on Sept. 11, 1996. On Sept. 11, 2001, she dedicated this poem to all the World Trade Center survivors:

Where do I start! Your world is in sudden turmoil, a passenger on a sailboat in the stormy ocean. The mercy of the swells. Your lives are changed forever.

Many strangers among you have a common bond. You will find comfort among them. They'll be a new extended family and new friends. Support each other.

Don't blame yourselves. Know this: that wherever you are, your loved one's spirits will be. Speak of them often. Write down memories and know they are safe, inside your hearts and minds.

- Jeanne
In Memory of Daniel

2.   Never Give Up: Bobby's Story

"I had to bring Bobby to this conference. I was afraid for him."
His three teenage children all died in separate car accidents, three
years in a row.

I have watched miracles happen, especially when parents who have lost a child are helped. This story is one of those miracles.

In July 2005, I attended the national Compassionate Friends Conference in Boston. I spend a lot of time in the bookstore selling my book. It was there I met Bobby and his sister when they bought my book. He was very quiet and withdrawn. She explained: "I had to bring Bobby here. I was afraid for him." In 2001, one of his teenage children died in a car accident. In 2002, the second of his teenage children died in a car accident. In 2003, the third and last of his children died in a car accident. All three children died in different types of car accidents. Bobby's wife was getting treatment in a special hospital.

"I love my brother and want to help him desperately," she said, "so I brought him here to hopefully get that help. I didn't know where else to turn, and I was very afraid for him and what he might do to himself. Bobby has always been a sweet, gentle man." No one should have to go through what Bobby has gone through; yet, it happens to the best of people.

Through the 3-day conference, I occasionally saw Bobby and his sister. At workshops, he sat quietly, taking in everything. His sister did a lot of talking. Gradually, at one of the evening sessions for those who had lost all their children, he began to talk also. Good for him, I remember saying to myself. You could see he wanted to talk, but held back for a while, not knowing how to start. Once he got out the first few sentences, it all flowed and he told his story. From that moment on, I could see a change in his demeanor, and I was happy for him. Perhaps, something was helping.

As things happen, I did not see Bobby again until the end of the conference when they both came into the bookstore to say goodbye. I gave them both a hug and then turned to Bobby and said, "I must ask you this. Was this conference of any help to you?" He looked at me and without hesitation said, "It saved my life."

Bobby was in a deep hole and never thought he could climb out. The fact that he did was a credit to his sister, the many people he met at the conference and the grief lessons he learned from all the speakers. Bobby went back home to North Carolina and started a Compassionate Friends chapter in his hometown where there was none and is now the chapter leader. The chapter is growing very strong and he can proudly say he did it all himself.

I lost track of Bobby for two years but constantly wondered how he was doing. Each time I spoke to a group I would tell Bobby's story. Most of the audiences had met him by then and knew exactly whom I was talking about, even though I never said his name. They all thought he was a very warm, kind man and wished him well.

Then at the 2007 national conference, both Bobby and his sister again walked into the bookstore. I recognized him immediately and smiled. What a powerful walk he had. What a powerful handshake. I could tell he indeed had come through the worst part. This does not mean he will not have any more bad times; he will probably always get teary-eyed when thinking of his children and talking to someone about them, but there is nothing wrong with that. After all these years, I still cannot mention my daughter's name without a little choke forming in the back of my throat and my eyes watering over.

We spoke, and I could see that indeed he had survived. His sister was glowing and very apparently proud of him.

The important lesson from this story is, of course, never to give up. Neither Bobby nor his sister did. They sought help and got it. What a credit to Compassionate Friends conferences and a beautiful example of how the workshops, the speakers and the sharing sessions have helped so many over the roughest parts of surviving grief.

3. A Positive Attitude: Diana's Story

Her son, Jimmy, died at age 10 of an accidental gunshot wound, while on a shooting expedition with his father and uncle.

In 2007, I invited a friend to dinner, Diana, who had been through hell and back. I wrote of her tragedy in my book *I Have No Intention of Saying Good-bye* and now it was 6 years later.

Her son, Jimmy, died in 1977 at age 10 of a gunshot wound, while on a shooting expedition with his father and Diana's brother. The brother, who was the cause of the accident, has never recovered himself and has had a difficult life since then.

Don't think for one minute Diana, or any other parent for that matter, would ever stop thinking about or grieving for that child, even after so many years! However, Diana is a survivor and moved on with her life, eventually divorced, and then was on the board of Compassionate Friends before becoming the executive director for 5 years.

"I did this in memory of my son," she said, and continues to honor him with all that she does now.

I lost track of Diana after she left that position, but in 2007, I planned a national conference in Scottsdale, AZ, for parents who had lost their only child or all their children and discovered in searching for a good speaker that Diana lived only a mile from me and was working for Hospice! She brought me up to date on her life which included her two other children who live in Arizona and California, her bouts with cancer, her heart attack, and her grief group meetings she held once a week.

On July 27, 2007, she became cancer free. Four days later on July 31, 2007, Arizona was deluged with one of the worst rainstorms in almost 100 years. Once again she was hit with a catastrophe...this time the rain turned into rushing currents and absolutely destroyed her house and everything in it including photos and lifelong keepsakes of her son Jimmy and her other children...things that cannot be replaced. "I was four feet in mud, without a home or clothing, and did not have flood insurance to cover this loss." (She was not in a flood area and didn't need to buy it.) Fortunately, my husband had a picture of Jimmy from the last conference, so at least we were able to replace a one of a kind, very precious item for her.

When she came to dinner later that month, she updated us on the previous few weeks, where she was living while her house was gutted and rebuilt and how she was trying to put her life back together once again. Her attitude was amazing. She laughed at things that would make me cry. She was thankful she wasn't at home when the rushing water came through her home and could have injured her severely. She was determined to get her life back together little by little and she did, even though she ended up having to walk away from her home because of lack of money to fix it.

Then additional heartache in 2009 when it was discovered one of her daughters had cancer. She took care of her for months and then lost her job with Hospice when job positions and layoffs abounded.

"Losing my income was very scary," she said. "I was on unemployment for almost a year. I knew I had to do something." That something was getting three part time jobs: a business she started where she cares for and supports seniors and those who care for them, another Hospice job with a new company, and a business venture she finds very rewarding. With these jobs, she believes she will be able to dig herself out of debt and be able to get back on track.

I again invited her to dinner recently for an update on her life and learned she is now in a better place mentally although her health is still a persistent problem. Her father died a year ago and she was able to retrieve items from her childhood she thought were lost forever. Her spirits are up once again and she believes the outlook is positive.

Diana is such an inspiration to people who are facing the loss of a loved one and although she no longer does the weekly grief workshops, she continues to speak to many groups and organizations on surviving grief and inspires others that there will be better days ahead.

I think we can all learn from Diana's experiences of how she lives her life. She is an enterprising person and continually positive, never giving up hope that tomorrow will be a better day. Everything she does is because of a little boy named Jimmy. She does it all in his memory.

4. Poetry For the Bereaved: Genesse's Story

"One of the miracles of poetry is that you discover what you didn't know about yourself... I knew I needed to learn how to express my feelings more to help others, instead of feeling sorry for myself."

Genesse Bourdeau Gentry, poet and author, wrote her second book in 2009 with both poetry and other narrative writings that look at expressing yourself in your grief journey.

She says, "One of the miracles of poetry is that you discover what you didn't know about yourself. I learned that one day joy and peace would come in and they have." Genesse's poems are simple, yet thought provoking. I find them easy to understand and can relate my own grief to many of them, as I am sure you would be able to also.

Genesse's daughter, Lori, died at age 21 in a car accident in 1991. She was completely devastated. "Everything I believed about life was tossed out the window, and I was filled with despair," she said. "It felt as if grief would destroy me. Friends didn't know what to do or say, often opting to do and say nothing."

According to Genesse, The Compassionate Friends is what saved her life. Through going to meetings, she discovered she could explain her feelings to others who understood. After a couple of years Genesse became a facilitator and discovered there was a whole new world of healing when she stopped going only for herself and began to attend meetings to help others, looking outside herself to give others hope.

"I discovered my own pain took a back seat to those newly bereaved," she said, "and from helping others, the words came in the form of poems about 2 ½ years after Lori's death." Genesse has one surviving daughter, Megan. Her first book "*Stars in the Deepest Night*" from 1993 is a collection of those poems, but she found she had more in her than she thought; in fact, enough for a second book.

The first poem she ever wrote is "Skin Deep," and is in her first book. "I wrote it in December, which is a difficult time of year for me because of the holidays and Lori's death. As the Northern California's regional coordinator for The Compassionate Friends, I knew I needed to learn how to express my feelings more to help others, instead of feeling sorry for myself."

Her latest collection of prose and poetry is in her book "*Catching the Light: coming back to life after the death of a child.*" The title is an interesting analogy. It relates to the fact that after tragedy huge enough to break us, to shatter the pieces of beautiful glass that were our lives, we have a choice. Let the glass stay broken on the ground, covering the graves of our dead lives forever, or pick up the fragments and put them together in a new way so we may heal and grow. "Since it can never be put back exactly like it was, the glass now has the potential to become a prism," said Genesse. "Instead of the light shining straight through us, it is captured by all our facets, each finely polished by our deepening into grief. As the fragments catch the light, more colors are revealed and rainbows are formed, reflecting all the colors of our lives."

For anyone who wants to start writing poetry, Genesse says you have to be open and understand where you are in your grief journey. Write down ideas as you think of them or they will be gone.

One poem she wrote, "Grief's Garden" is in both books. "The words came one night as I was going to bed. The poem is an explanation of how much work grief is for all of us and how you need to really feel the terrible things before the good things will come through."

In her newest book, a poem came to her much later on one Father's Day. She realized it was the anniversary of the last time she saw Lori, and the poem flowed out of her. The title is "*I Wonder*" and expresses how she, unknowingly, has grown in understanding her grief.

I Wonder

When did sadness stop covering everything?
I don't know.
It must have first been for moments,
then maybe hours,
days eventually.
Then for a long time
no longer ever-present,
but just below the surface
waiting for a thought to trigger it.
Now I live with more joy than sadness
but even now
sadness surfaces
unexpectedly
as the dark shape of loss
stirs the cauldron
and tears are added to the soup of life,
salty still,
but not as bitter
or overpowering,
adding an important flavor
to the whole of me.

Genesse has found purpose in her life, to help others in Lori's honor and to give them her gift…a gift of expressing yourself through poetry. You can find Genesse's books at www.afterthedeathofachild. com.

Note: the use of Genesse's last name was for contact purpose about her poetry books. I do not usually use last names in personal stories unless requested.

5. One Woman's Goal To Help Others: Carolyn's Story

The Project Smile outreach program, started in memory of son Stan, has helped thousands of poor children receive needed food, clothing and holiday gifts.

Carolyn, from Sugarland, Texas, a suburb of Houston, believes that it is her mission to keep her son Stan's memory alive through Project SMILE (Stan's Memory Includes Loving Everyone). Thousands of children and hundreds of senior citizens continue to be blessed because of Stan.

Stan died 26 years ago at age 17 when he fell off the back of a friend's car and severed the stem of his brain. He was, according to his mom Carolyn, a beautiful child, tall, blond, blue eyes, and a very sensitive and caring individual, from convincing his mom to help kids in a 5th grade class go to a special park for a special day of fun to making sure the man who loved his mom's banana pudding got fed.

"Stan always said that the important things in life are relationships, not material possessions or any other thing," Carolyn said. "He gave me more wonderful memories in his 17 years than a lot of mothers have in a whole lifetime."

What Carolyn does is appropriate to his memory, Project SMILE. This outreach program began in 1983, the year Stan died. One month before his death, Carolyn remembers taking Easter baskets to a youth shelter for poor children. She thought about it close to Christmas, called the shelter and got information about the children and their wish list spending Christmas Eve determined to brighten their bleak holiday. She reached out to 12 impoverished families from depressed areas in Richmond, Texas. The following year she went door to door in these depressed areas and helped even more people. "I found it very heartwarming to reach out to them in their need and in my grief," said Carolyn.

As time passed, service clubs like the Sugar Land Rotary Club and the Exchange Club of Sugar heard what she was doing and began helping her with both money and volunteer work. She spoke to various other organizations about the needs of many and about poverty. She says she has received letters from children who have said how much it helped their parents. One little boy said, "You're the best thing that ever happened to me. You knew just what I wanted. I really needed those socks."

This past year 3,368 children were helped, 1,227 with school supplies and the others with Christmas gifts, now known as Santa's Exchange. She does not solicit funds and says she gets more money for Christmas gifts, but school supplies are in great demand. In addition, she gets help from athletes, churches, businesses and ordinary citizens donating supplies and funds annually. When she has leftover holiday candy, she fills her car, drives to one of the neighborhood houses, opens her trunk and says, "Kids, go get your friends and come and get the candy." There is never anything left.

"This has been a beautiful outreach in Stan's memory and keeps me going," she says. It wasn't always like this. At first, Carolyn had a very hard time. She did not even want to wake up in the morning and face another day. Then a miracle came her way, a small grandnephew, named Cody that she took care of for his mom who worked.

"A lot of healing came those six years I kept him during the day for 8-10 hours," said Carolyn. "I was forced to focus on something else other than Stan. We had and still have a special love for each other. Cody, now grown, visits Carolyn often. He is a caring and sensitive person, and definitely helped me survive."

She thinks that God used Cody first and Project SMILE second to get her where she is today, in addition to a loving husband Carlos, Stan's stepdad, who begged her to make it through her grief journey. She says Stan's death did not affect him as badly as it did her, but realized much later on that he was in bad shape. "We would hold, cry and comfort each other." Carlos still works during the day but is supportive of what Carolyn does.

Carolyn also attributes her Christian faith as helping her a lot through her grief journey. "It has not erased any pain, but it has helped to make the pain bearable. Because of my faith in God, and Carlos' faith as well, my grief, although very intense and painful, is not without hope because I am confident that I will be with Stan for all eternity in heaven."

Carolyn, now almost 72, depends on volunteers but is responsible for keeping up with the families and making sure the information about them is correct. From 2001 – 2006 alone, Project SMILE helped over 14,000 children, according to Carolyn's figures. The numbers continue to rise. Approximately 2,000 children are her Project SMILE children and the rest are from the Women's Center and CASA.

In addition to receiving proclamations honoring her for her accomplishments, various governmental bodies honored her including the Texas State Senate as well as the highest award given by the Exchange Club, the Book of Golden Deeds.

Carolyn's loving spirit and dedication reflects the love she has for Stan, who would be very proud of his mom and her accomplishments. She encourages others who have lost children to find a project that will honor the child's memory and give a sense of purpose to the bereaved living in a world without their child.

6. Couples Deal With Grief Differently

*In my previous book I Have No Intention of Saying Good-bye I have three stories I find unique. All three stories deal with the death of **two** children, show how each family dealt with the loss, and how they moved on with their lives. These stories prove that no particular way is right in dealing with the death of a child. Each couple in this article chose what they felt was right for them and in the process was able to create a new normal, two of them with other children, one without.*

Bridie and Paul

Bridie and Paul lost two sons, one in a car accident, the other in a plane accident, almost two years apart. The story talks about their sons and the grief process they went through. They learned that husbands and wives grieve differently.

When the first son died, Bridie became involved with the son's friends who visited their home and found that how they handled death was fascinating. Paul, after a while, did not want them there. He felt intruded upon, whereas Bridie took great comfort in having them there. This was only one of many differences in their grief journey.

It took Paul a long time to function again at work, but he went back immediately. Bridie, on the other hand didn't go back for three months. Her mind wanted to shut down, physically and emotionally, but through it all, she became very spiritual. Unlike Bridie, when their second son died, Paul's anger turned to rage and consumed him for a very long time. Grief groups, friends and time eventually helped him. Bridie continued with grief groups long after Paul stopped and did not feel the anger he did and eventually went on a spiritual journey where she learned many things, helping her deal with both deaths and understand the reasons for all this. They still never go to the cemetery together, because of their separate reactions when there.

This couple's choice was not to have any other children, and they now lead rich, full lives and have done much to help bereaved parents by helping professionals understand us. When their sons died, they discovered that the medical community showed no caring attitude, no compassion. They began helping in an after-care program in trauma centers all over the country to teach professionals how to treat bereaved parents. They put on workshops, gave lectures and trained volunteers who help families going through a child's death. Both are well aware of how much the outpouring of love, which continues to this day, has helped them through their ordeal.

Joe and Wanda

Joe and Wanda lost two children, a boy and a girl, when a car driven by a 17-year-old smashed into theirs. Joe was Wanda's rock and stuck by her through all the bad times instead of throwing in the towel.

"We had a good marriage before the kids died, but our marriage became stronger afterwards," said Wanda. "If it wasn't for our faith or church, Joe and I couldn't have gotten through this. We are not over-religious, but we know with God's strength, we've come out on the other side. Even though at first we were angry at God for doing this to us, we know now He has carried us through these years and helped us."

Because of the great love they believed they still had inside them, they adopted a Korean child and are bringing him up. He is the love of their lives and their choice was to have someone to give all that love. They bring up this child to understand, love and respect the memory of the two children who died. They take him to the cemetery where he puts flowers on the stones and kisses the picture.

Joe and Wanda try to help other bereaved parents as much as possible. We try to tell them that it is important to understand husbands and wives grieve differently and to accept those differences within each other. What helped us most was having this strong faith, having each other, being patient with each other, going to support groups, doing memorials and talking to each other about the children. The more we talk about our children, the more it seems to help. It has made our journey a little easier.

Pat and Wayne

Pat and Wayne lost two children, a boy and a girl, in a horrific motorcycle/car accident. They began reluctantly going to grief groups and found it helped them. Others felt the same way they did at these meetings, they realized.

"I wanted Wayne to fix my broken heart and make everything normal again," said Pat. "I grew to expect that was his role. One day Wayne turned to me and said, "You know, it's hard for me to throw you a lifeline when I'm drowning myself."

"Those words were a real turning point," she added. "Grief is a selfish emotion. I realized then that I couldn't expect we would be grieving identically or that he could fix the unfixable. Those words turned things around and brought us closer together during this process."

What really helped the two of them most to cope with their loss was having more children. They had two, a boy and a girl. "Perhaps helping to cope with a death is the wrong reason to have subsequent children, but in our situation, we woke up one morning still feeling we were parents but not having anyone to parent," said Pat. "It was a lonely, awful feeling and a tremendous void. We had so much love to give."

They believe every couple has to decide for themselves what is right for them. They emphasize that the two children 'do not' and 'never could' replace the first two who died, but this new family talks about them all the time. The new children enjoy doing memorials during the year for their lost sister and brother, understand the situation and accept it.

Both also realized the need to help others. Pat is now the executive director of The Compassionate Friends national organization and Wayne helps by writing the magazine for TCF.

Three couples, three choices on how to survive the death of their children and move on with their lives. What is important to note is that everyone grieves differently, all have different ways of dealing with it and everyone is on their own timetable. These couples are content with the different choices they made, and they encourage others to seek answers in any way comfortable to them.

We will never know the happiness we once knew. However, it does become a different kind of joy; a joy filled with compassion, courage and the conviction that life is worth living. Each of these couples desires to help others. Trust your own timetable for healing, feel whatever you need or want to feel and you will grow in the process. I hope that you too, will reach new heights you never dreamed were possible.

7. Spiritual Bereavement Recovery: Christine's Story

"My work uniquely combines the spiritual and emotional aspects of grief to help you recover," said Christine.

Certified grief recovery specialist and bereaved mother, Christine Duminiak, facilitates Spiritual Bereavement Recovery that addresses both the emotional and spiritual sides of grief.

It means learning how to reclaim your inner peace and joy after an overwhelming loss so that you will be able to reinvest in and enjoy life once again. It includes learning how to express your innermost feelings and how to recognize your own direct and personal afterlife signs that you may be receiving from your loved ones, so you will know that they are ok and with God and are still a comforting part of your life.

"My work uniquely combines the spiritual and emotional aspects of grief to help you recover from your grief in a more holistic way," said Christine. "It includes your important ongoing connections to our loved ones and to a God who cares about your pain and loves you very much."

Christine is the founder of the world-wide non-denominational group called Prayer Wave for After-Death Communications and is the author of the spiritual bereavement self-help book *"God's Gift of Love: After-Death Communications--For Those Who Grieve."* She has been a featured guest speaker on many NBC affiliates around the country, in print media and has spoken to The Compassionate

Friends, MADD and other bereavement and support groups. She also co-hosts Ask the Angels on Blog Talk Radio. A new book *"Heaven Talks To Children"* is coming out.

"I have personally received many different types of afterlife contacts from my child and other members of my family who have died," she said. "Some of these were in the form of dreams, visions, coins, audio, music, butterflies, scents and touches. They were a key to my recovery." After-death communications occurs in these ways.

Estimations are that 20-40 percent of the population has experienced one or more after death communications (ADC). An ADC is an experience when a deceased family member or friend contacts you directly and spontaneously. It is without the use of psychics, mediums, rituals or devices of any kind. While some people contend that this is wish fulfillment, grief hallucinations or desires, those who have had the experiences believe they are real.

Others consider this moment as a "gift." According to research, the purpose of these visits and signs by those who have died is to offer comfort, reassurance and hope to their parents and other family members and friends.

Christine now does phone sessions with people who want help from experts in the field. She believes phone sessions can help release feelings, help learn after death contacts and signs of communication, help with guilt and forgiveness, learn a positive way of thinking about death, and learn positive steps to recovery.

Christine recommends the following spiritual books and her guided meditation CD to assist in your recovery in addition to her two books. They include:

"Hello From Heaven" by Bill and Judy Guggenheim
"Embraced by the Light" by Betty Eadie
"Love Lives On" by Louis LaGrand, Ph.D
"Glimpses of Heaven from the Angels Who Live There" by Sunny
    Welles

According to Marty Tousley, CNS-BC, FT, and grief counselor, a day at one of Christine's seminars she does with medium Sunny

Welles in all parts of the United States is a day filled with hope and love.

Christine emphasizes she is not a psychic or a medium, but can put you in touch with one. For additional information, email her at chrisduminiak@aol.com.

Note: Christine requested her last name be used for informational purposes and getting in touch with her.

8.   A Candle for Remembering Todd: Annette's Story

"When I awaken in the middle of the night, I can see Todd's light shining. I feel as if he is with me somehow, in the light of this candle."

Todd's mother, Annette, has found a way to remember her precious son all year long. It is as simple as placing a candle in the window. In her own words, she shares what she has done in his memory and dedicates this narrative to him and The Compassionate Friends, who taught her understanding, joy and a sense of serenity in knowing you are not alone in your grief. Others are walking with you on the road of life after the death of their children.

"Each night as darkness settles over our home, a little candle begins flickering in the east window of our staircase landing. The tiny light burns until dawn and then silently is quenched with the rising sun. This is my son's light. About a year after Todd died, I got a suggestion to place a candle in the window for the holidays, as I had no inclination to decorate.

I placed a candle there, and I have now replaced that candle with yet another candle. This is Todd's candle...this is Todd's light.

249

Todd's candle has a Victorian appearance and will burn steady or flicker. When the darkness comes forth, Todd's candle begins its nightly vigil...a vigil that will not end until I am dead.

Although this is a small gesture, it has deep meaning for me. Sometimes I awaken in the middle of the night and walk into the atrium at the foot of the steps to see the light of Todd's candle casting a gentle glow. I'll grab a glass of water and watch the candle flicker. Other times in the early evening, when only a reading lamp is lighting the living room, I will look into the atrium. Todd's light shines. I feel as if he is with me somehow, in the light of this little candle. I think about him, his life, his joys, his sorrows, and his immense capacity to love and to laugh. I feel a deep closeness to my son that cannot be explained to anyone but those who have lost a child. I understand that there is much peace and solace in keeping my child in my heart and life and in establishing my own private rituals of remembrance.

Leaving a candle in the window has been an American tradition since the Colonial Era. The candle symbolizes the warmth and security of the family home and its message is loyalty to a family member who is not present. Therefore, it is fitting that Todd's candle shines each night...reminding all that he is absent from our home, but not from our hearts.

Each of us has a ritual of remembrance of our child. Some of us have consciously established this. Others have unconsciously done so. This ritual brings our child close to us, only to us. Our rituals are a very personal choice. I chose not to share my ritual for 2 ½ years. One day a child who lives across the street asked me about the candle. I told her that it is my son's candle. She asked if he was in Iraq. "No," I said, "he's in heaven."

A momentary look of fright passed over her face, and then she smiled. "I thought you had kids. You act like a mom." Her innocent comment about me "acting like a mom" once again reinforced the fact that we will always be parents. Those of us who have children who have died will always be parents to those children. That role has shaped who we are, and intensified it more with the death of our precious child.

This is one element of losing a child that escapes the general population. If you have not lost a child, you don't understand, you can't understand the feelings and emotions that run so deeply in our psyches and our souls...We know what pure and overwhelming grief really is.

When I gaze at Todd's candle now, I remember his life, the security he felt within these walls, the growing up years, the love, loyalty and emotional stability he experienced as a child which enabled him to become a man of courage, self confidence and gentleness in the face of life's worst and best.

Todd's candle is one way to tell him that I love him as only a mother can love...unconditionally and forever. I will always remember. I will always be Todd's mom.

I have found that being a parent is a lifetime journey...even when our children are not with us on life's road. As parents, we define ourselves as interwoven with the fabric of our children's lives. We always remember. There is comfort in that."

9. The Choking Game: Ken's Story

"I put this choking game up there with drugs and alcohol. It needs to be classified with other risky behavior and identified as such."

Ken's 15-year-old teen son Kevin died in 2009, when he played the choking game (aptly named suffocation roulette) and lost. This is where players intentionally choke themselves until they pass out temporarily. It is a brief sense of euphoria, and sadly, teenage kids like Kevin think it's safe. Unfortunately, that is not true. Many have died each year; others thankfully have survived, some still in a coma.

"We thought an awful lot of kids were committing suicide by hanging recently," said Ken. "Now we are thinking maybe it was this game, not suicide at all. They never thought they would die."

A recent Oregon study of 10,000 kids showed that over 36 percent have heard about this "game" and 1 in 5 has tried it.

The anger was overwhelming. Ken says his remaining family prays a lot, stays close, talks to each other and is healing as a family. They are also going forward and trying to educate the public.

Ken's mission is to now travel around the country and speak to various high school groups and anyone that will listen. "I've found teens to be overwhelmingly supportive," he said. "They want to know good information and thank us for telling them. They say they didn't realize the danger and now know what to look for."

Most parents have never heard of the choking game. They are reluctant to address this issue and are in denial for two reasons. First, they say, "Not my kid. He/she wouldn't do it. He/she knows better." Second, the parents say, "If we tell them about it, they'll try it, so better to keep it quiet." According to Ken, parents need to educate their kids on the danger of this so-called game. If you want kids to make informed decisions, they've got to know the truth and the consequences. It is fear that causes inaction.

Warning signs that this is happening to a teen are marks on the neck, changes in behavior, bloodshot eyes, disorientation at strange times, withdrawal, sudden drop in grades and finding ropes and belts all over their room.

"I put this choking game up there with drugs and alcohol. It needs to be classified with other risky behavior and identified as such," said Ken.

Ken believes that talking about this helps to heal his heart. "Having kids come up and thank him for information is the greatest reward he gets," he says. "When I stand before God and my son, I will not be trying to explain why I idly stood by and let this happen to others. I'm not going to do that. I am going to take advantage of the opportunities sent to me. That's my goal. We owe it to every parent to do what we can to save our children."

"These kids are playing a game where there are no winners, and they should be aware of that," he said.

10. Reinvesting In Life: Kay and Rodney's Story

From the devastation of losing their daughter and finally renewal, this couple decided to start a national organization for parents who have lost their only child or all their children, Alive Alone.

Reinvesting in life is what Kay and Rodney Bevington, bereaved parents, have chosen to do since the death of their only child, Rhonda, in 1980.

"By reinvesting you can commemorate your loved one by taking memories of the past and the love that you shared into the future," said Kay. "It keeps their memory alive and gives meaning and purpose to our lives as it can for yours."

Kay would like bereaved parents to think of an organization or institution, what they need and what parents can do for them in memory of their child. "It doesn't have to be lots of money. It can just be buying a uniform for a child for a sports team or band or donating books to the library of a school or planting trees in a schoolyard. Take the interest of your child and what they liked to do or enjoyed being around, and you will find something that would be a reinvestment."

"Don't try to do this in the first part of your grief journey," she said. "You need to do your grief work first. Then you will be able to think of how to commemorate your loved one."

As an example of one of their reinvestments to honor Rhonda is two $1,000 scholarships they give for a student's freshman year of college. Sixty students have received assistance since Rhonda's death. The Rhonda Kay Bevington Memorial Scholarship is given each spring based on Christian character and leadership to two students who are members of either the high school or church where she attended. Some of these recipients are now the parents of students who are receiving the grants or applying for this award. Kay and Rodney have also purchased theater seats at their local performing arts center in memory of Rhonda and donated to the Hospice Center in Van Wert, OH, in her memory.

Rhonda, almost 16 when she died, had a chronic cough in the spring of 1980 along with laryngitis that led to pneumonia and put her in the hospital for a while. The cough persisted, and doctors decided to do a CAT scan. They thought they saw a mass behind one of her lungs and decided to do what they thought to be a routine biopsy. She had a capillary collapse during her four-hour surgery and died soon after. Later they found she had Lymphoma and it was expanding into her lungs, closing off oxygen she needed to survive.

"At no time did anyone say the surgery was life threatening," said Kay. "If we had done nothing, the doctors said she would have died from coughing and eventually choking to death."

"I was a teacher at the time, took off a month after her death, and upon my return told my classes there would be times I would cry and leave the room to get myself back together. They reacted well and were supportive. Young people are more comfortable and open with death than many adults. A teacher friend who had also lost a child several years prior was my support system and the students were so loving and kind that it gave me a reason to get out of bed each morning. I had to concentrate when at school and school gave me a diversion and brief respite for a few hours. I honestly feel now, in retrospect, that these students also saved my life with their love and acceptance.

"When I would go home after teaching, the house was like a morgue and the silence was deafening," said Kay. "I had no desire to cook, clean or keep anything organized at home.

I also had difficulty sleeping; I didn't take care of myself; I didn't exercise. Yet I felt this intense need to create so I did crafts and baked lots of food for other people. I remember cooking for Rodney and being upset that he seemed to enjoy eating. I lost weight and had no desire to eat."

Rhonda and her parents got along well and spent a lot of time together. Kay says she was the center of their lives. Rhonda told Kay she was her mother, her sister and her best friend. Their lives revolved around Rhonda and all of her activities, interests and organizations with which she was involved. "Rhonda made us a family where previously we were just a couple. So when she died we had to reinvent our marriage and our lives."

"I felt that I wanted to die when Rhonda died, said Kay. "I wanted to be with her and I didn't care that my husband, friends, family or my school children needed me. I only wanted to be with her. I had a wish that the world would end because my world had ended. I never proceeded to act on this wish, but I distinctly remember the feeling."

She also read anything on grief she could get her hands on, but in 1980, there was nothing out there except Harriet Schiff's "*The Bereaved Parent.*" Today there are tons of books and materials to help any bereaved parent.

Many men hide their feelings as they go through the grief process. "Rodney seemed to function on automatic pilot and continued to work and never showed any emotion after Rhonda died. He hurt as much as I did, but in a very different way. He thought he had to hold it all together as I fell apart. He never cried, and I cried all the time. He told me if I didn't stop crying everywhere we went he would quit going with me places. He read nothing about grief. I wanted to attend every bereavement meeting available and he wanted nothing to do with it. I talked about Rhonda all the time; he listened but rarely initiated conversations about Rhonda."

Seven months after Rhonda died Kay forced Rodney to go with her to the local chapter of Compassionate Friends (TCF) meeting that the two of them and another couple started. "Attending these meetings and being editor of the newsletter saved me from self-destruction and saved our marriage as we began to understand how men and women grieve differently," she said. Rodney gradually began to talk about Rhonda, shared his grief with his co-workers and no longer balked about attending support group meetings. We no longer began to accuse each other of grieving improperly and gave each other permission to grieve in our own way and on our own timetable."

Rodney completed some of Rhonda's needlework during this period, which he had never done previously or since. He wanted to complete things that she was robbed the opportunity of doing. He now says he does not know how he did it, as that is not a talent or interest of his.

One of the most difficult things she and Rodney have encountered is when people would say to her, "Why don't you have other children?" They discussed adoption of an older child since at the time of Rhonda's death they were thirty-nine and forty-one, but realized they were too old to start once again by having another biological child, even if it had been possible. They talked to others who, unfortunately, had bad experiences with adoption, and also realized they needed to do their grief work first and by then would be too old to adopt.

"Sometime between three to five years I slowly realized we were going to live and we had to make a decision about the quality of life we wanted," she said. "We decided that we wanted to keep Rhonda's memory and the love we shared with her in our hearts and minds as well as others. I knew we would never be the same people we were before this happened." She still encourages her friends to talk about Rhonda, and when friends send a holiday card, to put something in it about Rhonda and ask others to share memories also through cards. She received cards and gifts for a long time and one friend every year gives Kay a rose bush to plant.

Kay says there are unique aspects of being a bereaved parent of an only child. They include:

- having no one to reinvest your love or energy in anymore
- who do you celebrate holidays with
- what do you do with the child's possessions
- having someone to take care of us when we get older and be our advocate
- not having anyone to call us at holidays such as Mother's Day or Father's Day or Christmas

- attending family reunions where no one but yourself and your spouse are there
- changing your will
- listening to people talk about grandchildren, but never having any, unless your child was older and married.

"These things make us different and that is why it's so important to connect with others like ourselves and create a networking system so that we have people to call or visit."

From this devastation and renewal, Kay and Rodney decided to start an organization for parents who had lost their only child or all their children. Alive Alone was born and recognized throughout the world for support given to these parents. A periodical is published five times a year, parents are networked according to the age and cause of death of their children, speakers for bereavement conferences come from this group and they support the endeavors of several to plan and organize special gatherings and conferences. There are, however, no Alive Alone chapters in each city, only the national organization. The website to access for other information is www.alivealone.org. Kay answers all emails personally.

Kay and Rodney still attend many bereavement conferences annually and provide support for these parents with a unique need that is often not recognized or understood in the bereavement community. Kay speaks at TCF, Bereaved Parents USA, and Parents of Murdered Children (POMC) annually. She also is the author of two books and the TCF brochure "*The Death of an Only Child.*"

Kay and Rodney are shining examples of the good that can come out of devastation and when they look back, they can be proud of their lifetime accomplishments.

Note: Kay and Rodney requested their last name be used for informational purposes and getting in touch with them for information on Alive Alone.

Part 6

Book Recommendations

Many good books of a personal or very general nature are available for your perusal. In this section of my personal recommendations, one may find books by mothers who want to share their stories, by fathers who want to express their pain and by religious leaders and others who want you to take a closer look at the role of God in all this. Each book can help guide you through your grief journey and explore the changes within you, or you may find others not listed just as helpful. In the end, we learn that no one ever fully recovers, but instead, learns to live and accept their child's death and moves on with their lives.

The grief over lost children never dies;
it is a grief that relents only a little.
And then only after a long time.

- John Irving

1. Books That Offer Comfort To Bereaved

Books offer comfort, and many times the right words, to many who grieve the loss of a child. Until the early 1990's there was not much available, but now there are many good books published. The following titles are just some of the wide variety that, over the years, remain popular with bereaved parents.

No Time for Goodbyes by Janice Harris Lord was the first book I received and read. This book is about coping with sorrow, anger and injustice after a tragic death. In my case, it was a sudden car accident. Mothers Against Drunk Driving (MADD) recommends this book, and since a friend of mine was one of the state directors at the time, she literally rushed it over to me. As I read it, I felt I could identify with many aspects of the book and would underline, star and circle particular passages that I wanted to come back to and resembled my feelings exactly. Most of all, it made me feel not so alone in my grief, just knowing that others felt the same as I did. The book became a substitute for a grief group with its practical information about loss and grief. As one person said, "It puts into words the heartbreak and utter devastation we feel when a loved one has been suddenly taken from us in any form of death."

The Bereaved Parent by Harriet Schiff finally brought grief of a child into the spotlight. Hiding your grief under the table was how you dealt with it until then. This break-through book offers guidance to the bereaved and systematic suggestions on how to cope with the stages of grief, from the funeral to rebuilding your marriage.

Letters to My Son by Mitch Carmody is a compelling story of love, loss and recovery through letters and poems that Mitch wrote as a catharsis for his grief over the death of his 9-year-old son following the son's battle with brain cancer.

The Worst Loss by Barbara Rosof talks about how families heal from the death of a child. She delves into explaining about grief and how all family members grieve differently. She draws on personal stories and research and has different families speak about all types of deaths and planning what you can do with the rest of your life.

How to Survive the Loss of a Child by Catherine Sanders talks about rebuilding your life and filling the emptiness with joy again. She also has a chapter about how friends and family members provide the best support. Special cases of miscarriage, stillbirth and induced abortion are also covered.

After the Death of a Child by Ann Finkbeiner discusses living with loss through the years, a book that examines the long-term nature of parental grief through the words of those who suffered through it.

A Broken Heart Still Beats, After Your Child Dies by Anne McCracken and Mary Semel offers comfort in the voices of other writers, many of them famous authors. Anne and Mary's reflections of their own losses introduce each chapter as they look at literature as medicine, stories and poems by authors themselves.

Singing Lessons by singer Judy Collins is a memoir showing us the depth to which her soul is shaken when her son commits suicide, how her exterior was shattered and the interior made vulnerable and raw. "It is like a wound," she says, "that opens up so we can feel and experience the depths and then climb to heights never imagined." This book is a moving account of growth and healing, dreams and meditations imbued with the introspection we love in her songs. Judy emerged on top, keeping her heart open and her life in harmony. She and I spoke of our losses after a brilliant speech I listened to which ended in the singing of one of her trademark songs, "Amazing Grace."

Saving Graces by Elizabeth Edwards explores Elizabeth's entire life, but concentrates on the death of her teen son in a car accident and how the "community" of people in her life, friends and strangers, helped her to find solace and strength she never knew she had in order to deal with her son's death and her own subsequent tragic illness. I was fortunate enough to meet and speak to this lovely woman in 2007, and I know that whatever she says about her life and feelings comes from a strong, courageous heart that I completely admire.

Comfort by author Ann Hood, whose raw emotional experience of how she felt after losing her daughter to an illness is hauntingly reminiscent of my own feelings after my daughter died. There is something very special about an autobiography that allows you into the author's soul to feel every feeling the author feels. I understand those feelings because I have been there too. I met this lovely woman in 2008 and listened to her story as she eloquently spoke of her child, Grace. This book is the sequel to her first bereavement book *The Knitting Circle,* also a good read on how knitting saved her life after her child's death.

First You Die by Marie Levine takes you on her grief journey after learning of the death of her only child. She does this in essays, poems and prose revealing how the anger and denial turns to the courage and strength it took to learn to live again.

Catching the Light-Coming Back to Life after the Death of a Child and **Stars in the Deepest Night** by Genesse Bourdeau Gentry are her two poetry books expressing her profound love for her daughter. She portrays a parent's horrific grief experience at the loss of a child and the long journey to healing. Genesse hopes these poems will give others solace and help them realize they are not alone. She writes the prose sections eloquently.

Beyond Tears: Living After Losing a Child by Ellen Mitchell is about nine mothers who lost children in their teens or young adults. These mothers talk of the shock, agony and desperation of the first year and how they have coped since.

Into the Valley and Out Again by Richard Edler is about his son dying. Rich's life seemed to stop and it took him a few years to climb out of the bottom of the valley of grief he had never encountered before. By the end of the book, he understands acceptance, sorrow, faith and what is important in life. Unfortunately, Rich died far too young, but his prolific writings will live on and continue to help those in need.

Roses in December by Marilyn Heavilin reaches out to help those who are grieving find God's comfort. After losing her three sons and still surviving, Marilyn understands the sorrows, struggles and questions that come. She shares how even in the winters of our lives God provides roses, those special occasions, people and memories, to give us strength to persevere. She also talks about the grieving process of family members and siblings.

When Bad Things Happen to Good People by Rabbi Harold S. Kushner tells of his 3-year-old son, diagnosed with a fatal degenerative disease. Rabbi Kushner asks God, "Why me?" In this book, he shares his wisdom as a rabbi, a parent and a human being as he delves into his many questions of God and his wisdom.

The Other Side of Grief by Darcie Sims and Alicia Sims Franklin answers many questions asked by bereaved parents such as "How long will my grief last?" "What is on the other side of grief?" and "How will I know when I am better? Explore the changes you go through while on your grief journey.

When the Bough Breaks by Judith Bernstein takes us through bereaved parents' stories to offer comfort to those still navigating this journey, no matter the cause. We learn that no one recovers from this devastation, but learns to live with it and move on. The book is divided into two parts. The first is "The Way through Mourning" and discusses factors that shape mourning and the nature of the death. Part 2 looks at "The Rest of Our Lives: Altered Perspectives" and discusses marriages, family relationships and spirituality.

Remembering with Love compiled by Elizabeth Levang and Sherokee Ilse takes each emotion, quotes a real person and discusses through poetry and prose why we feel the way we do after a loved one dies. The messages of hope at the end of each page can apply to any loss.

Love Never Dies by Sandy Goodman takes us on a grief journey through her private pain to a place that she understands the love you lost will remain with you in many different ways. For anyone on the path of spiritual growth and enlightenment, this book will open your heart and mind to understand the journey is never over.

My Son...My Son: A Guide to Healing After Death, Loss or Suicide by Iris Bolton is a personal story dealing with Iris' son's suicide and how she survived the nightmare. She shares her experience, describes the tortured process and the reactions of those left behind. She offers messages of hope and healing for others in similar situations.

When Every Day Matters: A Mother's Memoir on Love, Loss and Life by Mary Jane Hurley Brant poignantly shares her daughter Katie's courageous battle with brain cancer and how she coped with the loss. Besides being an author, Mary Jane is also a psychotherapist and grief specialist.

God Is Bigger Than Your Grief by author Karen Tripp delves into the mysterious realm of faith and the questions we have in dealing with our heartache over the death of a loved one, particularly, in our case, a child. Interspersed with personal stories from those who have gone through the bereavement, she believes we can learn new ways to soar as we draw closer to God and realize he is always with us and has a purpose for everything.

God's Gift of Love: After-Death Communications...For Those Who Grieve and **Heaven Talks To Children**, both by Christine Duminiak are spiritual bereavement self-help books about afterlife contacts from our children and ongoing connections to God. Her books address both the emotional and spiritual sides of grief.

I Have No Intention of Saying Good-bye is my first grief book. In it I share 25 stories from bereaved parents who open their hearts about their courage, hope and attempts to make sense out of the most unbearable loss of all, that of a child.

Books on specific causes of death like SIDS or AIDS are also available. There is a wealth of information to help all of us through our grief journey. Take advantage of these literary works.

2. *Where To Purchase Bereavement Books*

The Centering Corporation (www.centering.org) provides education on grief and loss for professionals and the families they serve. It now has a compilation of over 500 resources for grief and loss including its own magazine Grief Digest. They continue to provide educational offerings, bookstores, and workshops for caregivers and families, with a heritage of becoming the largest provider of resources for grief and loss in the nation. Their books are not only available online but also at many national bereavement conferences held around the country.

Barnes and Noble (www.bn.com) and **Amazon** (www.amazon.com) will also have the majority of grief books available to the public. Go to the sites, type in the name of the book and you can order them online. It only takes a few days to get them.

Any Major Bookstore Chain or Independent Bookstore in your city will have grief books available or can order them from the publishers directly.

Part 7

Resources for dealing with grief recovery

When a child dies, we have questions of where to go for help and to whom we can turn. In this computer age, resources are easy to find, and there are many. Three main national support groups I list are a good start. They can direct you to other specific sources, depending on the type of death and other circumstances. In recent years, web site support groups allow parents to sit in their homes and be part of an online group or a chat room. Many parents find it more comfortable if they can deal with their grief in a way that allows them privacy. Know that whatever road you choose, someone will be there to offer comfort and a friendly hand.

Hope smiles in the threshold of the year to come,
whispering that it will be happier.

- Afred Lord Tennyson

1. *General Bereavement Support Groups*

The Compassionate Friends (http://www.compassionatefriends.org) is for bereaved parents, siblings and grandparents. Local groups meet one or two times a month where all can come to talk or just listen to others with guidance from those who have been there before. It provides support, reading materials and a yearly national conference with workshops on more than a hundred topics. Phone number is 1-877-969-0010.

Alive Alone (http://www.alivealone.org) is specifically for parents who have lost their only child or all their children. There are no local meetings, but Kay Bevington, who heads the organization, sends out newsletters to share grief thoughts written by bereaved parents and keeps everyone informed of conferences across the country, including if there are any for the Now Childless parents. She also has books and videos where experts guide bereaved parents. Contact Kay at 1112 Champaign Drive, Van Wert, OH, 45891 or through email at alivalon@bright.net.

BPUSA- Bereaved Parent USA (http://www.bereavedparentsusa.org) provides a network of peer support groups, newsletters and help for parents, grandparents and siblings. It is very similar to Compassionate Friends but on a smaller scale. Phone number is 708-748-7672.

2. Specific Bereavement Support Groups

ISA- International Stillbirth Alliance (www.stillbirthalliance.org), also known as *First Candle* (www.firstcandle.org) is a non-profit coalition of organizations dedicated to understanding the causes and prevention of stillbirths, including miscarriages and ectopic pregnancies, making up a large percentage of these causes. Their mission is to raise awareness, educate on recommended precautionary practices and facilitate research on the prevention of stillbirth. ISA serves as a centralized resource for sharing information and connecting organizations and individuals. Phone number is 1-800-221-7437.

The American Society of Suicidology (www.suicidology.org) supplies information to lead families of suicide victims to local resources such as survivor's groups. Phone number is 202-237-2280. One of these groups is The Samaritans (www.samaritansri.org) which provides self-help support. They hold meetings every week to allow the opportunity to ventilate feelings. The national hotline is 401-272-4044

The Candlelighters Childhood Cancer Foundation (www. candlelighters.org) is for parent support of children who have or who have had any form of cancer. It is worldwide; there are no dues; they do have a monthly newsletter. Their philosophy is that "It is better to light one candle than to curse the darkness." Phone number is 301-962-3520.

SIDS- *The National Sudden Infant Death Foundation* helps parents deal with the shock and grief of losing their babies to SIDS and connects those parents. It provides information and counseling services and has a bimonthly free newsletter. Phone number is 301-322-2620.

The National Association of People with AIDS (www.napwa.org) educates the public and provides services needed for those afflicted with AIDS. They can also refer people to additional sources of help. Phone number is 240-247-0880.

Parents of Murdered Children (www.pomc.com) puts grieving parents in touch with each other. There are chapters all over the United States for support and you can be with those who will listen and understand. Phone number is 513-721-LOVE (5683).

TAPS- Tragedy Assistance Program for Survivors (www.taps.org) offers peer support and assists survivors who have lost a loved one in the line of military duty. They also have a national magazine published during the year with interesting stories of hope and survival. In the summer, they sponsor a "good grief" camp for children who lost a parent or sibling. Phone number is 1-800-959-TAPS (8277).

MADD- Mothers Against Drunk Driving (www.madd.org) educates the public about the dangers of drinking and driving. They work to get stronger laws passed against drunk drivers. A quarterly newsletter is available. Phone number is 1-800-GET-MADD (438-6233).

National Hospice and Palliative Care Organization (www.nhpco. org) provides individual help as well as group therapy to the bereaved. Books and information is available for bereaved of all ages. Phone number is 703-837-1500.

National Tay-Sachs and Allied Diseases Association, Inc. (www. ntsad.org) helps parents with literature, emotional support and talking to parents with similar experiences. Phone number is 1-800-906-8723.

3. Web Site Bereavement Support

The Open to Hope Foundation (www.opentohope.com) and *The Grief Blog* (www.thegriefblog.com) help to connect all those who have suffered a loss and to provide expert as well as peer-to-peer resources to help with the grieving process. There is a specific section for "death of a child" on the Open to Hope site, where articles are written to help the bereaved cope with their pain and find hope for the future. The Foundation has expanded its online channels to include Facebook, Twitter and YouTube. Dr. Gloria Horsley and Dr. Heidi Horsley, both professional therapists, started the Foundation.

Healing the Grieving Heart (www.health.voiceamerica.com) is a bereavement program at 9 a.m. pacific time every Thursday on the web. The show features Dr. Gloria Horsley and Dr. Heidi Horsley. The popular, ongoing series keys in on issues of importance to families that have experienced the death of a child as well as other losses. Each week an interview is conducted with a professional therapist, author or parent.

Angel Moms (www.angelmoms.com) chat daily, sharing tears and laughter. Through their pain, these mothers have bonded together to offer each other love, support and understanding, something we all need.

My Child Loss (www.mychildlossgrief.org) has lots of information, tools for grieving parents, phone support, and a place to leave comments and messages. Their first goal is to bring members together for a retreat to promote wellness and facilitate healing through interactive workshops, speakers and relaxation. The second goal is to educate society about parental grief, including ways to support and respond appropriately to grieving parents. Lastly, they want to educate employers about parental grief and encourage them to offer more leniencies toward their employed bereaved parents.

Fernside Online (http://www.fernside.org) is a non-profit, non-denominational organization serving grieving children and their families. This site encourages sharing stories, feelings, and memories with trusted friends, honoring the search for new beginnings.

Hygeia (http://www.hygeiafoundation.org) is an online journal for pregnancy and neonatal loss, one that can give hope to many.

MISS-Mothers in Support and Sympathy (http://www.misschildren. org) is an organization with the mission of providing a safe haven for parents to share their grief after the death of a child. The emphasis is on support for the entire family.

Angel Child Legacies (http://www.angelchild.com) site offers parents the opportunity to celebrate the life of their child or children by submitting the child's legacy to the site. They also offer help with saying "just the right thing."

Angel Hugs (http://www.angelfire.com/or/angelhugs) offers real help to get through the bad times like holidays, birthdays, death anniversaries, and family gatherings. It includes a "photo tribute" to "our beautiful kids" and "stories from heaven."

Miscarriage Support and Informational Resources (http://www. fertilityplus.org/faq/miscarriage/resources.html) offers support for women who have suffered a miscarriage. Information is through the comprehensive list of chats, newsgroups, books and more.

Virtual Memorials (http://www.virtualmemorials.com) create memorials that celebrate the lives and personalities of those lost. It also provides a place where these cherished images and biographies will have a permanent home.

Journey of Hearts: (http://www.journeyofhearts.org) invites you to join the journey of recovering from losses and significant life changes – a process that does not occur overnight. Journey of Hearts is a healing place with resources and support to help those in the grief process following a loss or a significant life change. This site offers something for anyone bereaved.

The Grief Warehouse (http://www.griefwarehouse.org) is for parents who are coping with the death of their child. The goal is to be a warehouse of information and personal experiences…a place where you can come, gather ideas, and share what worked for you on your journey of grief.

Angels of Addiction (http://www.angelsofaddiction.com) offers support and help to the addict and support for bereaved families and friends.

GriefNet.Org (www.griefnet.org) is an internet community of persons dealing with grief, death and major loss. They have 37 email support groups and 2 web sites. They provide help to people working through loss and grief issues of all kinds. Support groups include accidents, only child, suicide, SIDS, substance abusers among others. More descriptions are on the web site.

Grief Loss and Recovery (www.grieflossrecovery.com) offers online grief support through an email discussion group (list serve). The group offers emotional support and friendship and provides a safe haven for bereaved persons to share their grief.

SIDSID (PSC@Home.Ease.Lsoft.com) is an email support for SIDS and Infant Death. To subscribe, send an email to *ListServ@home. ease.lsoft.com*. In the body of the email type: SUBSCRIBE SIDSID – PSC

Loss of a Child: to subscribe to this list, send an email to *lossofachild@ onelist.com.* In the body of the email, type *lossofachild-subscribe@ onelist.com.* This list is for those families who have lost a child due to tragedy or illness. This list serves as a support group to help get through this most difficult time.

TCF Atlanta (http://www.tcfatlanta.org) is a group of parents who want to help in any way they can, and they are doing it on a popular web site that offers support, information, an online newsletter, poetry, memorial sites, reading suggestions, stories from the heart and much more.

The Cope Foundation (www.copefoundation.org) is a grief and healing organization dedicated to helping parents and families living with the loss of a child. Since 2000, COPE (Connecting Our Paths Eternally) has connected individuals who have experienced similar losses by providing ongoing emotional, therapeutic and spiritual programs. These include parent and sibling support group meetings monthly, weekly art and movement therapy workshops, and a variety of special programs for members mourning a child's passing, as well as the community.

Rowan Tree Foundation (www.rowantreefoundation.org) is a non-profit organization providing support to families that have suffered a prenatal or infant loss. Based in Colorado, they have a variety of activities planned throughout the year including a butterfly release, a charity benefit, a candlelight remembrance and an annual walk to remember the children.

Grief, Inc. (www.griefinc.com) provides seminars, trainings, community seminars, books, tapes and more than 30 years of experience helping others light the candle of hope after the death of a loved one. Darcie and Alicia Sims are recognized international speakers on the topics of grief and grief support as well as Tony Sims, a nationally known presenter and management consultant.

Facebook, Twitter *and* **YouTube** are now places on the internet you can go to as an outlet for grieving. People the world over can post messages, photos and videos. The Web has put grievers in touch with all sorts of people who can help support them through the pain.

4. Chat Rooms for the Bereaved

GROWW (www.groww.org/chat/gr.shtml) offers a grief recovery chat room that is open 24/7. They also host many types of moderated grief support chats. Peer groups teach that you have permission to grieve. It is also a place of belonging and one helps you to get through the pain so you, in turn, can help others.

The Compassionate Friends
(www.compassionatefriends.org/chat/chat_entrances.shtml) The organization offers multiple bereavement support chats. These are scheduled, facilitated live chats for grieving family members with such topics as parent/grandparent bereavement, bereaved two years and under, bereaved over two years, pregnancy/infant loss, sibling support and survivors of suicide.

iVillage/parentsPlace (www.parentsplace.com/chat) has an extensive chat schedule that includes a variety of chats on parenting. There is at least one chat for bereaved parents to help them work through their grief.

Part 8

Closing Thoughts

My wish for all bereaved parents in the world is to find comfort, hope and the courage to face your tragedy in the days, weeks, months and years to come. In doing so, you will come out on the other side of grief. In this final section, I first reflect on my present husband and second, on my daughter in another poem dedication. In a postscript to my first husband, who was very special to Marcy, I thank him for helping me bring her up to be a fine human being.

What do we live for if not to make life less difficult for each other.

- George Eliot

1. *The Greatest Gift*

Each day I have to reflect on how lucky I am. Lucky to have a partner, my husband, who is so loving, so caring, so full of life, so willing to be helpful in anything I need, and most of all, so understanding of me and my loss, the greatest loss of all…that of a child. I dedicate this page to you, Lawrence.

My husband makes sure I never forget those special days that are important to all bereaved parents. He has everything marked down in his PDA, birthdays, death anniversaries, special ceremonies. When those days arrive, we do something special. Either we light a candle and he says a short prayer, or we might go somewhere where someone is honoring the lost children. Every few months he says, "It's time to go to the cemetery, visit Marcy and bring flowers." I agree with a smile, happy that he wants to make the journey with me. We always make time in our busy lives to go together.

If I have a bad day…and after all this time there are still and always will be bad days…he hugs me for as long as I need him to. He cries with me also. When we talk to others about Marcy, he gets very emotional. I watch him in awe. Here is a man, who, unfortunately, never knew my daughter (she died nine years before he and I met), yet it is as if he feels everything I feel and more. He speaks of her lovingly as though she were part of him.

It is too bad they never met. They would have really loved each other. Marcy, too, was a giver, a sweet person who always tried to look for the good in everyone, who was always there to help a friend, and who was loving to everyone around her.

Every day he makes me laugh. He tells me a joke or does something funny. He thanks me for laughing at his old jokes. (I don't know they are old…and I do think they are funny!) Laughter is the most important medicine you can take. Laughter opens up your heart, makes you breathe easier, and gives you hope that today will be a good one. He says, "I love to hear you laugh. I hope a little laughter pushes out some of the sadness in your heart." It does help.

We have not known each other very long, but it's as though he has been part of my life forever. I love you, Lawrence. You are by far the best thing that has ever happened to me. Thank you for being who you are and for loving me, the greatest gift you could ever give me.

I hope you all have special people in your life to love and comfort you in times of happiness and in times of sorrow.

2.   Hope Poem

My hope: that each of you will find peace in your heart, joy with your families and hope for the future. I write and dedicate this poem to my daughter, Marcy.

HOPE

As I look up to the sky,
a bright star shines down.
I feel it is you smiling at me,
telling me it is okay for me to laugh,
it is okay for me to be happy again.
I'm trying, I tell you.
It is not an easy road to travel
when you have lost the most
important thing in your life.
But my heart is full with love
from a wonderful man and many friends.
And, of course, I feel your love surround me
on this chilly December day.
It warms my heart and my body as always.
I keep busy and try to make a difference
in this world by helping others.
I do it for you, in your memory,
and I find it is a wonderful feeling.
I know you used to do it also,
you used to help close friends
and even strangers.
I look around me and see young people

enjoying the outdoors, running, playing,
wishing for a good snowfall.
I hear their laughter and their good wishes.
I know there is hope for a better
world when I look into their eyes.
I wish I could share everything I say
and do with you, as I used to.
I miss you so much,
my beautiful daughter.
I think of you every minute of every
day and always will.
I want you to know, though,
that I was always a survivor
and will continue to be one
both for you and for me.
I love you, always and forever.
Mom

3. Postscript

On the day I was to send this manuscript to my publisher, Marcy's father, Jess, died from medical complications. It was a shock and unexpected and in that respect similar to Marcy's sudden death.

Jess was a kind, loving individual, and although we grew apart and divorced many years before, we remained friends. One of the reasons was Marcy. We joined together to bring her up and watched her grow into a special person. We were always able to talk about her as no other two people could. He would mention Marcy in speeches he gave and whenever talking to friends or anyone who knew her. I still try to do the same. We never want to forget her, nor do we want others to either.

At the beginning of February 2010, Jess became part of the bereavement group I started in Scottsdale and was very enthusiastic about playing a major part in helping others in hopes of also helping himself. He was one of those who had a lot of trouble getting through the grief process and I, too, was hopeful this would help him. It was not to be.

I hope he is at peace now. I am sure he and Marcy are hugging and laughing at a funny story he is telling her. They both had a terrific sense of humor. Goodbye, Jess, and thank you for helping me give life to Marcy, our most prized accomplishment.

CPSIA information can be obtained at www.ICGtesting.com
Printed in the USA
LVOW061910021112

305624LV00003B/60/P